CAN YOU
TRUST
the BIBLE?

Harold J. Sala, PhD

ROSE
PUBLISHING

If you are looking for a life-changing confidence lifter on the Word of God, this is a book for you. I know of no more helpful bridge to confidence in the Christian life than the truth expressed in this book, linking apologetic evidence and practical Christian living.

NORMAN L. GEISLER, PHD
Author/Apologist/Co-founder of two seminaries

Supported by both scholarly evidence and engaging illustrations and examples, Dr. Harold Sala, who I respect and admire, has compiled a thorough resource that will answer your questions and renew your faith in the Holy Bible and give you the confidence you need to stand up to the challenges against Biblical truth and authenticity. I especially loved that Dr. Sala has included very powerful life changing testimonies and has given every reader a practical approach to Bible study. Clearly explained, comprehensive and helpful; this book is a must read.

GREG LAURIE
Pastor/Evangelist Harvest Christian Fellowship

Dr. Sala has a wonderful gift for teaching timeless precepts from God's Word in a way that makes the most profound ideas very simple to grasp—and even very difficult truth is irresistibly sweet. In this excellent work, he explains why Scripture is trustworthy and why it is important to embrace—and obey—the truth of the Bible. I love his infectious joy and confidence in God's Word. This book is a real treasure.

JOHN MACARTHUR, LITTD, DD
President, Master's College and Seminary,
Pastor and Bible Teacher

Harold Sala rightly observes that though the Bible is a bestseller year after year it is seen as irrelevant for many because they do not consider God as its author and guide—and consequently, of their own lives as well. Sala combines scholarly research with fascinating historical illustrations to uncover a book that has shaped the lives of countless over the centuries and one that has life-changing relevance for today. I commend his work to you with much appreciation for his insight.

RAVI ZACHARIAS
Author and Speaker

Here is a practical book that shows how and why what we believe should make a difference in the way we live. Drawing on years of experience, the author helps us get inside both the Scriptures and our hearts to show us what transformed living is all about.

ERWIN W. LUTZER, THM, LLD
Author / Pastor Emeritus,
Moody Memorial Church, Chicago

Can You Trust the Bible?
Copyright © 2020 Harold J. Sala

Published by Rose Publishing
An imprint of Hendrickson Publishing Group
Rose Publishing, LLC
P.O. Box 3473
Peabody, Massachusetts 01961-3473 USA
www.hendricksonpublishinggroup.com

ISBN 978-1-62862-964-4

All rights reserved. No part of this work may be reproduced or transmitted in any form or by any means, electronic or mechanical, including photocopying, recording, or by any information storage and retrieval system, without permission in writing from the publisher.

All Scripture quotations, unless otherwise indicated, are taken from the Holy Bible, New International Version®, NIV®. Copyright ©1973, 1978, 1984, 2011 by Biblica, Inc.™ Used by permission of Zondervan. All rights reserved worldwide. www.zondervan.com The "NIV" and "New International Version" are trademarks registered in the United States Patent and Trademark Office by Biblica, Inc.™

Scripture marked (GW) is taken from GOD'S WORD®, ©1995 God's Word to the Nations. Used by permission of God's Word Mission Society.

Verses marked NKJV are taken from the New King James Version®. Copyright ©1982 by Thomas Nelson. Used by permission. All rights reserved.

Verses marked KJV are taken from the King James Version of the Bible.

Scripture quotations marked (NASB) are taken from the New American Standard Bible® (NASB), Copyright © 1960, 1962, 1963, 1968, 1971, 1972, 1973, 1975, 1977, 1995 by The Lockman Foundation. Used by permission. www.Lockman. org

The statements and opinions expressed in this book are solely those of the author and do not necessarily reflect the views of Rose Publishing, LLC or that of its affiliates. Citation of a work does not mean endorsement of all its contents or of other works by the same author(s).

Printed in the United States of America
010620VP

CONTENTS

ACKNOWLEDGMENTS

Like most authors, I have written this book standing on the shoulders of a significant number of individuals who gave of themselves in helping me develop a love for the Bible and understand its true greatness and uniqueness. I am indebted to them not only because of the knowledge they conveyed in a classroom, but also because of the manner in which they shared their hearts and lives one-on-one and lived out the message they espoused.

I am also grateful to Thurman Wisdom, who carefully evaluated the chapter on manuscripts, as well as Elizabeth Trever, the wife of the first American to see the very important Isaiah manuscript found in Qumran. She graciously met with me, giving me personal insights about the intriguing drama that unfolded when God allowed centuries-old manuscripts to escape their dark hiding places to emerge in a twentieth-century world dominated by scientific skepticism.

My thanks also go to the men who graciously endorsed this book and the publisher, whose faith in the subject I've written about cements a common bond of understanding.

CAN THIS BOOK
BE TRUSTED?

The truth is that the light which shines in this
incredible book simply cannot be put out.
Malcolm Muggeridge

The Bible has been translated into literally thousands of languages. A knowledge of this book has been an integral part of Western education and has played a prominent part in society and civilization. A portion of the book of Psalms was the first work to be printed with movable type by the German inventor Johann Gutenberg in Mainz, Germany around the year 1450.

In 1971, when astronaut Ed Mitchell went into space as part of the crew of Apollo 14, he took with him the first book to go into space—a Bible. It was a small piece of microfilm about two and a half inches square, having been reduced 62,000 times, containing the 773,746 words of the King James Version of the Bible. It could easily be read, provided the reader wore glasses with the ability to magnify the text 100 times.

American presidents take the oath of office swearing to uphold the Constitution as they place one hand on the Bible and raise the other hand, affirming, "So help me God."

During the Holocaust, tens of thousands of men and women went to their deaths quoting the words of Psalm 23, "The LORD is my shepherd," or Psalm 91, "Whoever dwells in the shelter of the Most High will rest in the shadow of the Almighty." Untold millions of people pray, "Our Father in heaven, hallowed be your name," or quote the great chapter on love found in 1 Corinthians 13.

In 1968, an American naval vessel strayed into territorial waters claimed by North Korea, and a handful of North Korean soldiers took the vessel. Aboard were seventy crew members and seven officers. What followed was described by some of the men as eleven months of hell. After a few weeks of captivity, the men began to put together a Bible of sorts—pieces of toilet paper with as many verses of Scripture written on them as could be cited from memory. The toilet-paper Bible was then circulated among the men for comfort and strength. I suspect that there were some pretty strange omissions and revisions of the text, but the words brought comfort and hope to the prisoners.

Researcher George Barna contends that ninety-three percent of us own Bibles, yet less than half of those who own one ever read it. Another researcher, George Gallup

Jr., agrees with him. As the result of his research, he says, "People revere the Bible, but they don't read it—that's what it comes down to."

You can be ignorant about many things and get along quite nicely. You can hire technicians to fix your computer, ask specialists to diagnose and cure your medical problems, hire consultants and marketing experts, tap think tanks, and find people who know what you don't; but when you have an ignorance of the Bible, you are vulnerable to a host of doubts, conjectures, and uncertainties regarding some of the great issues of life.

Why Is This Book Important?

Consider the fact that no other book in the entire world:

1. Introduces you to a God who is a loving Father—not an angry deity—who loves you, will forgive you, and will embrace you as his child in spite of your failures.

2. Gives you a history of humankind from the time of creation.

3. Contains hundreds of fleshed-out prophecies telling how the great drama of the ages will be played out, articulating the flow of nations, armies, and history.

4. Makes claims to uniqueness and authority as does no other book ever written.

5. Answers the most important questions that arise from the human heart:

   ○ Who am I?

   ○ Where did I come from?

   ○ Why was I created?

   ○ Where do I go after I die?

   ○ What should I value?

6. Provides a basis and foundation for your faith.

7. Brings you comfort in times of sorrow and encouragement in times of difficulty.

8. Gives you hope that there is life beyond the grave and that heaven is a reality.

9. Shows you God's purpose and will for your life.

10. Produces benevolence and charity in the lives of those who practice its teaching.

Many people today, if asked whether or not they believe the Bible, would quickly say, "Yes, of course, I believe the Bible," but acknowledging it as authoritative with regard to their conduct is another matter.

In the realm of faith, the matter of authority is a red-hot issue. Who says that you should believe this or disbelieve that? By whose authority do you challenge long-held beliefs and practices? Why are you a Christian and not a Buddhist, or a Muslim, or an animist? Why do you believe what you believe?

In recent years, however, the belief that the Bible is true and should be accepted as authoritative has been widely challenged by a skeptical, unbelieving mindset. In this book, I present six powerful reasons why you can accept the reality that the Bible is a God-given book, unlike any other religious document in all history. In his ministry, Jesus was never taken aback by individuals who came with sincere questions. Nor is God offended, I believe, when you sincerely come to him and ask him to show you whether or not he is the truth.

Find out for yourself what makes the Bible worthy of your trust!

Let's get started.

THE UNIQUENESS
OF THE BIBLE

*The highest proof of Scripture is derived in general
from the fact that God in person speaks in it.*
John Calvin

The Bible Is Unique in Its Authorship

James Henry Breasted, an authority on ancient civilizations, authored one of the few high school textbooks that made a lasting impression on me, a thick textbook titled *Ancient Near Eastern Civilization*. Breasted was the first American to ever earn a PhD in Egyptology and the one credited with coining the oft-used term "Fertile Crescent" to describe the span of civilization reaching from Egypt to Mesopotamia.

Breasted, whose picture appeared on the cover of Time magazine on December 14, 1931,[1] was a scholarly forerunner of the Indiana Jones-type archaeologist. He wrote factually, but with such exuberance and excitement that I devoured his book. It made me want to take a shovel and personally go exploring myself. Visiting the Museum of Egyptian Antiquities in Cairo years later, I recall the artifacts were exactly as the pictures I had seen in vivid black and white in the textbook.

I remember with fascination how Breasted described the first written documents ever found, having been originally written in the Tigris-Euphrates River valley near the Sumerian states of Kish and Ur. Those first documents were pretty common, garden-variety sort of writings—deeds to property, inventory lists, and even marriage covenants. Breasted contended, as do most scholars today, that writing began about 4000 BC, though no one knows exactly how it evolved. At first, pictures or marks represented words, which were gradually accepted in a certain geographic area and became standardized. Carbon ink was used to inscribe pottery or stones and, by the year 3000 BC, writing was common.

Writing on Stone

Preceding the production of papyri in Egypt, a method of pictorial writing had been developed in Egypt known as hieroglyphs. Tombs and monuments record the exploits of pharaohs with this picture-writing "based on a complicated system of consonants."[2] Babylonians did the same thing. About 1750 BC—some 300 years before Moses wrote, "In the beginning, God created the heavens and the earth"—Hammurabi, the Babylonian king, appointed stone masons to produce a stele (an upright stone monument) with 250 laws. It was massive—about seven and a half feet in height and six feet in width, with the laws carefully inscribed. Visit the Louvre Museum in Paris and you can see it for yourself, with its rules and its punishments if those rules were broken.

Hammurabi's law code included provisions for all kinds of injustices—repayment of thefts, agricultural rights, the rights of slaves, children, women, individuals who had been injured, injustices, and compensation for murder.

Papyrus: Paper of Ancient Egypt

About 3000 BC (and perhaps even a long while before that—nobody knows for sure), Egyptians discovered a use for papyrus, a reed which grew along the banks of the Nile. It could be cut and placed in strips, with a secondary layer of strips being placed on top perpendicular to the first layer, then rolled firmly and dried.

From this they made such diverse products as boats (the basket in which baby Moses was placed along the Nile was probably made of papyrus), sandals, fuel, tables, and chairs. And far more important, especially in relationship to the Bible, was that papyrus was suitable for writing materials. The Egyptians thus gave the world the substance that would eventually be used in the libraries of the world, with papyrus sheets being joined into scrolls.[3]

The book of Job speaks of papyrus, asking, "Can papyrus grow tall where there is no marsh? Can reeds thrive without water? While still growing and uncut, they wither more quickly than grass" (Job 8:11–12).

Each year the banks of the Nile overflowed, flooding surrounding marshes where papyrus grew in abundance; but without the marshes, there would be no papyrus, reasoned the writer. He also points out the weakness of the substance—it is organic and, in its natural environment without water, the reed quickly withers and dies. It was this writing material that was used to record much of the original manuscripts of Scripture. Because it lacks the durability of a piece of clay or the hide of an animal, papyrus is subject to disintegration and decay and thus eventually becomes unreadable.

Moses wrote the Ten Commandments on tablets of stone, but in all probability the Bible as we know it was first written on papyri. This also explains why those original documents have long since disintegrated—but fortunately, not before they were accurately copied and preserved for us today.

Should you have an opportunity to visit Cairo, you will find numerous museums where you will see what was used for the centuries-old process of making writing materials from papyrus.

The Birth of the Bible

Surprising as it may be to some, the Bible was not the first document to be written, although it is the oldest surviving book in print. But it is the first book ever written that comprehensively began with creation and provided a history of God, man, and the devil, with implications for how these truths relate to present-day living. It also contains clearly outlined prophecies extending to the time when God says, "Enough!" and calls a halt to life as we know it.

Who Wrote the Bible and How Were They Qualified?

The simple answer is that about forty individuals wrote the manuscripts and documents that we now call the Bible (a word that came from the Greek word *biblia*, meaning "books" or "scrolls").[4]

What were their qualifications and backgrounds? A study of their lives shows vast differences in education levels, backgrounds, places in society, and even abilities.

- Some were simple laborers, such as Amos, who tended sycamore trees, and Peter, James, and John, who were fishermen.

- Some were priests who had studied the Scriptures and had received a theological education.

- Some were men with either direct or indirect connections to royalty. Moses was the adopted son of an Egyptian princess and received the finest tutoring and education that ancient Egypt could provide.[5] David and Solomon were kings. Isaiah, possibly a cousin to the king, had access to the royal court.

- One was a physician from Syria, probably the only gentile who contributed to the Bible. As the author of the gospel that bears his name and the book of Acts, Luke was the largest single contributor (in volume of what he wrote) to the New Testament.

- Then there was the rabbi turned evangelist, Saul, whose name was changed to Paul, who wrote thirteen letters to various groups/persons. He was the theologian of the New Testament, a man destined to greatness even if he had never been converted on the road to Damascus.

- Another was a tax collector, Matthew, who was sitting at his table in the customs house when Jesus called him. He eventually wrote the first gospel.

How does one account for the fact that so many different individuals could write about God, history, and religious beliefs and yet all their writings reflect essential harmony, unless they had been guided by an unseen hand

and power? That is exactly what the Bible contends. That influence, according to Peter, was the Holy Spirit. Peter stated, "Prophets, though human, spoke from God as they were carried along by the Holy Spirit" (2 Peter 1:21).

To understand the implications of the complexity and enormity of this, visualize the following: Suppose that forty individuals from all over the world were summoned by the director of the Hermitage Museum in St. Petersburg, Russia. Their assignment was to find a piece of marble in any shape or color and to bring it to the museum on a specific date. Generally, there could be no communication between these individuals. Most of them had no idea that someone else was involved in this project. Then upon the given day, the various pieces of marble were unveiled. Some were quite small. Others were very large and had to be transported by trucks or flown in by cargo jet. A few of the pieces were brilliantly colored. Others were opaque and lighter in shades and colors, yet when the individual pieces of marble were put together in a kind of jigsaw puzzle, a beautiful mosaic took shape revealing a beautiful scene. Talk about a miracle! Such would be added to the Seven Wonders of the World and people would come from far and wide to see this phenomenon.

Here's the analogy: Some portions of the Bible are short—Philemon and the second and third letters of John are only a few verses in length. Others are lengthy (have you ever wondered when you would get through the "so and so begat so and so's" in the Old Testament genealogies?). Yet the documents comprising the Bible fuse together in a marvelous pattern of God's love for humankind and his refusal to let them turn and walk away from him.

Also significant is that what they wrote blends in literary harmony. Going back to the analogy of forty individuals who are summoned to bring a piece of marble to a great museum, let's suppose that on these pieces of marble they are to write their thoughts about God, humankind, where civilization is headed, and, perhaps, a brief history of the world. Can you conceive of anything as I have described having a sense of meaning or continuity unless what was written was supernaturally directed? At this point you are forced to recognize the preposterously stacked odds against this having just happened, and you are confronted with the supernatural character of the book.

Speaking specifically of the Old Testament Scriptures, Paul says, "All Scripture is God-breathed and is useful for teaching, rebuking, correcting and training in righteousness" (2 Timothy 3:16). Another version puts it this way: "All Scripture is inspired by God." It should be noted, observes Norman Geisler, that the "single time the New Testament used the word *inspiration*, it is applied only to the writings and not the writers."[6]

How did this inspiration affect the outcome of what was written? Were the writers simply scribes who mechanically wrote what God dictated, or did their personalities and individuality come through? A careful study of the biblical books shows their individuality in the way they wrote and expressed thoughts and ideas. Even though their literary styles differed, there was a mystical supercedence that rendered their words as the words of God himself. Their writings bore his stamp. Erwin Lutzer explains, "Inspiration does not just mean that God approved of their writings, but that men actually wrote his words. His ideas became their ideas, and they accurately recorded what he wanted us to know."[7]

The record of what the Bible teaches is inspired and authoritative. Scripture contains the factual recording of many kinds of evil and violent deeds—certainly deserving of an "R" (restricted) film rating. But it truthfully and accurately conveys what happened so that we can benefit and learn from the mistakes of others.

When Was the Bible Written?

The Bible came together over a period of fourteen centuries—a fact so enormous that it almost defies belief. How so? Ideologies and accepted popular wisdom changed from generation to generation and from century to century. Yet, no one revised what had previously been written in Scripture in order to make it harmonize with the latest documents.

Moses wrote the first five books of the Old Testament, known as the Pentateuch (literally from two Greek words, *pente* meaning "five" and *teuchos* meaning "tool[s]," hence, the five books of the law). Jews refer to the same thing as the Torah. Historians date the giving of the law at about 1400 BC.

These five books were not God's first revelation of himself and his plan for humankind. They were, however, the first written record. God revealed much about his plan and purpose for humanity to the descendants of Adam and Eve, and these stories were passed from generation to generation—an oral history. Some stories, such as the account of the Flood, were duly retold in different cultures and geographic localities.

The Bible itself bears witness to its distinctive and unusual authorship. When the books of the Old Testament were written, they were immediately recognized as the Word of God. Hundreds of times, the Old Testament writers rang out the words, "Thus says the LORD." More than sixty times the New Testament asserts, "It is written!" That was their source of unquestioned authority. They knew what had given these documents validity—the voice of God on the mountain, accompanied by the bolts of lightning and the clap of thunder. Isaiah wrote, "The grass withers, the flower fades, but the word of our God stands forever" (Isaiah 40:8 NKJV).

There is little evidence that anyone in ancient days questioned the authority of the Hebrew Old Testament. Men may have ignored it, spurned it, and violated its teaching, but they knew it was the Word of God. When Jesus was here, he fully accepted the authority of these books we call the Old Testament. He said, "One jot or one tittle shall in no wise pass from the law, till all be fulfilled" (Matthew 5:18 KJV). Those somewhat strange English words "jot" and "tittle" referred to the smallest strokes of a pen in writing two Hebrew letters. The NIV translates this passage as: "Not the smallest letter, not the least stroke of a pen, will by any means disappear from the Law until everything is accomplished." Jesus had no intention of taking the smorgasbord approach of sifting what he liked and rejecting the rest.

The New Testament church fully accepted the authority of the books which came from the pens of the Old Testament writers of Scripture. Both Jesus and Paul quoted Moses, recognizing his authorship as the writer of the first five books of the Bible.

Following the recording of the first book of the Bible, other books were added. Some were history and some were poetry. Other books were largely prophetic in nature. But all had the ring of authenticity. Those scrolls were collected by scribes and considered to be sacred.

God gave humankind this book because he wanted to communicate his love to the world, and it follows that he would do so in languages that were widely used and understood at the time. This meant that Hebrew was the primary language of the Old Testament, and a type of Greek known as *Koine* (a street version of the language used in the marketplace and by millions of people throughout the then-known world) became the language of the New Testament.[8]

When a need arose for the Bible to be translated, because groups of people no longer knew Hebrew or Greek, translations were undertaken, now numbering in the thousands. The Bible has been translated into more languages than any other book in all of history and continues to be the world's most widely distributed book.

The Bible Is Unique in Its Structure

One of football's greatest coaches, Vince Lombardi, would begin every season by holding a football in his hands. He would then address his players, many of whom were seasoned veterans, and say, "This is a football!" Of course, they knew it was a football. They had been kicking and tossing one since they were kids. Why state something so obvious? He was stressing that fundamentals need to be re-emphasized.

Open a Bible and you will immediately recognize it is a single book, but divided into two parts, which we call the Old Testament and the New Testament. While the two are separated by some 400 years, they are as integrally connected as the two hemispheres of your brain. Both function together. St. Augustine said the Old Testament is unveiled in the New Testament. Or as others have put it, "the New is in the Old concealed, and the Old is in the New revealed."[9]

The Bible Is an Anthology of Books

In the Old Testament you will find the law that God gave through Moses, historical books, beautiful poetry, and prophecy (some call them major prophets and minor prophets—based on the length of the book, not the importance).

In the New Testament you find biographies of the life of Jesus; the continuation of the infant church established on the day of Pentecost; the teaching of Paul and others, which explains how to apply the truth of the gospels to our lives and world; and finally, a thrilling book of prophecy culminating with Armageddon and the return of Jesus Christ to establish his kingdom forever.

In spite of the popular terminology referring to the Old and New Testaments, it would have been more descriptive to call them the Old and New Covenants. (The word covenant, *diatheke* in Greek, notes an agreement between two individuals or parties.) The first describes the agreement or covenant God made with the patriarchs: Abraham, Isaac, and Jacob, and their descendants. But the second represents the covenant that God made with humankind based upon the sacrifice of God's Son, Jesus Christ, who paid the price for the redemption of humanity. The New Covenant is about God's relationship with his people following the coming of Jesus Christ.

It is comforting to know that the Sovereign God who created the universe cares enough about his subjects to enter into an agreement that he is bound by his character to honor and that his Word will not be broken. As the Puritan scholar Perry Miller put it: "When you have a covenant with God, you no longer have an ineffable, remote, unapproachable deity; you have a God you can count on."[10]

The following is an overview of most English Bibles.[11]

OLD TESTAMENT		NEW TESTAMENT	
Law	Law – 5	Gospels – 4	Narration
Prophets	History – 12	History – 1	Continuation
Writings	Poetry – 5	Letters – 21 (13 + 8)	Explanation
Former	Major Prophets – 5	Prophecy – 1	Consummation
Latter	Minor Prophets – 12		
	39 Books	27 Books	
Here's how to remember:	3 x 9 = 27	39 + 27 = 66	The Traditional Bible

The Bible Is Unique in Its Claims

Peter says that the Bible did not originate with men; rather, men wrote as they were "carried along" by the Holy Spirit. Paul affirms the same thing, saying, "All Scripture is God-breathed." To suggest, as some do, that some portions of Scripture are inspired while others are not leaves us in a quandary: Who is to determine what is inspired and what is not? Are we to presume that the parts we like are "inspired," but when some parts bother us, we throw those to the trash heap?

Consider some of the statements the Bible makes about itself:

> The grass withers and the flowers fall,
> but the word of our God endures forever.
> (Isaiah 40:8)

Forever is a long, long time! When you are a kid, "forever" is the length of a church service, or the duration of the school term, or the length of time that it takes for the dentist to drill out your cavity, but the concept is time without end. The Hebrew word translated "forever," which is incidentally the same word translated "eternal" in the next passage, means "to veil from sight" or "to conceal." Isaiah used the word to contrast the fragility of a rose or a flower that fades with the certainty that the Word will endure the unrelenting assaults of its detractors and have no end.

Your word, O LORD, is eternal;
it stands firm in the heavens.
(Psalm 119:89)

The psalmist suggests that God's directions and counsel recorded in Scripture originated in his presence and will stand the test of time. The word that the psalmist used that is translated "stands firm," *natsab*, means "established" or "fixed." The same word was used of a monument that had been firmly planted in the ground—one firmly established. *Smith's Bible Dictionary* says the same word was used of a well-fortified army garrison. It was also used of a "column erected in an enemy's country as a token of conquest" (1 Samuel 13:3).

"Truly I tell you, until heaven and earth
disappear, not the smallest letter,
not the least stroke of a pen,
will by any means disappear from the Law
until everything is accomplished."
(Matthew 5:18)

An illustration from the Hebrew text to which Jesus was referring gives meaning to what he said. The phrase translated "the smallest letter" (Hebrew *yod*) was the tenth letter of the Hebrew alphabet. It was the equivalent of the Greek *iota* (again, the smallest letter of the Greek alphabet—the equivalent of an apostrophe). And the second phrase, "least stroke of a pen" or "tittle" (as translated in the King James Version), can be illustrated as follows using the Hebrew letter *daleth*.

The slight extension of the horizontal line crossing the vertical one is known as the *keraia*. It was the omission that Jesus was speaking of. Was Jesus speaking in hyperbolic terms, exaggerating to make a point? No. But he was making a strong argument—one they understood much better than we do today. He was saying, "Scripture will be fulfilled exactly as it is written!" English translation cannot demonstrate how the slightest stroke of a copyist's pen can completely change the meaning of a word. For example, compare the following Hebrew words and how they are translated.

to praise   **to profane**

The only visual difference in how they are formed is the slightest stroke of pen closing the left hand leg of the radical. But the two words stand in opposition when it comes to their meaning.

In our generation, passages such as that written by Peter about the heavens and the earth passing away with a great noise and the earth melting with fervent heat didn't mean much until the atomic era was ushered in on the gleaming wings of science. What appeared to be hyperbole during Peter's time comes within the range of possibility every time the doors to the nuclear silos are rattled and a nation threatens to start the nuclear chain reaction. What Peter wrote could easily play out in the context of today's nuclear world. Did Peter understand the scope of what he was writing? Probably not, but God did.

"Heaven and earth will pass away, but my words will never pass away." (Matthew 24:35)

Both this statement and the previous one were made by Jesus Christ. Scholars are in agreement: No other religious document in the entire world makes such claims. "What about the Koran?" you may ask. Are such dogmatic claims made by its writer? An English translation of the Koran tells you what it says in direct terms. (Incidentally, Islamic scholars say that unless you read and understand Arabic, you cannot appreciate the beauty of the Koran). But even an internet concordance of the book shows no claims such as those made by Jesus Christ as recorded in the New Testament.

"If you risk asking the hard questions of the Koran," says Ravi Zacharias, "you risk being branded, and, in some cases, you even risk your life. The Christian, however, has always been willing to subject the Bible to the severest analysis and is able to come out, knowing that it can survive the blade of the skeptic."[12]

> For the word of God is alive and active.
> Sharper than any double-edged sword,
> it penetrates even to dividing soul and spirit,
> joints and marrow; it judges the thoughts
> and attitudes of the heart.
> (Hebrews 4:12)

The contention of the writer of Hebrews is that *the Bible is alive!* How so? It has a way of penetrating our hearts and minds, quickening us to the truth of what God says and orders for our lives. It convicts, reproves, guides, and comforts.

Accepting the fact that the Bible is given by God gives it uniqueness and, far more important than this, it gives authority to the words you read on the pages of this grand old book.

The Bible Is Unique in Its Formation

From the moment ink dried on a papyrus scroll to the printing of the Bible that you read, three steps or progressions over a long period of time can be observed in relation to the Bible's creation.

STEP 1: Revelation by God

God, not wanting humankind to walk in darkness, revealed something of himself to his spokesmen (known as prophets), who then recorded the revelation. Sixty-one times in the Old Testament you will find the phrase, "The word of the Lord came to me . . . " The prophet Jeremiah uses it ten times. He specifies "a second time," and so forth. At times he was a reluctant recipient of the Word. He made excuses, pleading that he was just a youth, but when God revealed something or spoke through him, it was immediately recognized as the Word of the Lord by those who heard or read it.

When Moses came down from Mount Sinai, his face was so bright with the glory of God that he had to cover his face. There was no question in anyone's mind. They knew that God had spoken and that what Moses brought down, written with the finger of God on those stone tablets, was his Word. Moses was God's spokesman. When his sister, Miriam, challenged his authority, she was struck with leprosy—an evident token of God's displeasure with her challenge.

Forty-eight times in thirty chapters, Ezekiel, a prophet in exile in Babylon, uses the same phrase: "The word of the LORD came to me . . . " It was a powerful connection with heaven, and people listened.

STEP 2: Reception by Men

The second part of this transaction is that God's Word was received by humankind. And how did people know whether or not God, in fact, spoke through the prophet? Moses gave them a very simple test: Did what the prophet say that God revealed happen? If it didn't, then what should happen to the prophet? "But a prophet who presumes to speak in my name anything I have not commanded, or a prophet who speaks in the name of other gods, is to be put to death" (Deuteronomy 18:20). Strong penalties for those who faked revelations from God!

Revelation from God resulted in reception by people, accompanied by the recognition that God had indeed spoken through the prophet, priest, psalmist, or writer. But one more step follows.

STEP 3: The Collection and Preservation of the Text of Scripture

By 400 BC, the Old Testament in the form we presently know had come together. It is nothing less than astounding that it has endured the test of time without corruption and loss.

The collection of New Testament documents is a story that is both complex and less clearly defined than that of the Old Testament. Open a New Testament and the first four books you find are known as gospels. Actually there is but one Gospel—that is the Good News[13] of what Jesus said and did, though it is recorded by four individuals. We know them as Matthew, Mark, Luke, and John.

These four accounts, however, were not written in the order they appear in your Bible. In all probability Matthew was the first to write an account of the life of Christ, followed by Luke, then Mark, and finally John.[14] Why the order in which they appear in your New Testament? Because of the common themes or subject matter.

The first three—Matthew, Mark, and Luke—are known as the "synoptic" gospels, a term that simply means they told the same story from three different viewpoints. Matthew (the tax collector Jesus called as he sat at the table of tax collections) is the most Jewish of the three, and his account is considered generally as the most chronological. Writing from a Jewish standpoint, he portrays Jesus as the long-awaited Messiah.

Mark, on the other hand, is writing from a Roman viewpoint. His book, which is marked with a staccato speed, is sometimes referred to as "the Businessman's Gospel." Throughout the book, he sprinkles the Greek word *euthys*, meaning, "straight-away, immediately, or forthwith." The sixteen chapters in this book are filled with exciting events. What happened in the ministry of Jesus was what Mark focused on in his writing. It is quite likely that Peter dictated much of what Mark recorded.

Luke, a Syrian physician, writes with a tenderness that reflects his personal training and compassion. He specifically mentions the place women had in the ministry of Jesus and paints the passion of Christ very vividly. In his book, Jesus is the perfect man, appealing to the Greek mentality.

John—unlike the first three—singles out twenty-one days in the life of our Lord and focuses on the events that take place at that time. Chapter thirteen through the end of the book focuses on the last seven days in the life of Jesus Christ.

After the gospels comes the book of Acts. It details the continuation of the life of the early church, recording the three great missionary journeys of Paul, but stopping quite abruptly with Paul under house arrest in Rome, leaving the impression that there may be more that was originally written but did not survive.

Twenty-one letters (thirteen by Paul) and eight others known as general letters or epistles (an old term that simply means "letters") provide instruction and guidance for the lives of men and women who were struggling with what it means to be a Christian in a non-Christian world.

Then John, writing from exile on the island of Patmos, penned the book we know as Revelation, bringing to a close the twenty-seven books which were eventually recognized as the New Testament.

A final disclaimer: When John put down his quill pen, he didn't breath with a sigh of relief and say, "Whew! That's it, now let's rush this to the printer." It took quite a long period of time for these twenty-seven documents to be recognized as being those bearing the stamp of authenticity and genuineness. The process of how these books gained universal acceptance is a story I'll tell in Chapter 3.

The Bible Is Unique in Its Preservation

No other book in all history has been so revered, so cherished, and so copied as the book we know as the Bible. More than 20,000 ancient manuscripts of various parts of the Bible exist today[15]—a vast number including over 5,300 ancient Greek manuscripts, 8,000 manuscripts of a Latin translation of the Bible, over 1,000 manuscripts of various translations, and thousands of biblical quotations found in the writings of the early church fathers.

Before movable type was perfected in the 1440s by Johann Gutenberg, the Scriptures were copied by hand. It was painstaking, laborious work. Often scrolls were made in a kind of classroom known as a Scriptorium. The instructor would sit at the front of desks where scribes would carefully, word for word, write down what was read or dictated by the instructor. It was serious business.

Should a mistake be made, scrolls were often given ceremonial burial—something that has provided rich resources for subsequent generations when they were later discovered. When a scroll became too old to be of use, it was also buried or burned.

Ancient rabbis have related that when Scripture was being copied, even if a king should walk into the room, the scribe would not rise until he had completed the portion he was copying, reasoning that the king was mortal—he would eventually die, but God's Word was sacred and would endure the test of time.

The Contribution of the Masoretes

The Hebrew word for "tradition" is *Massorah*; hence the term "Masoretes"—a group to whom a debt of gratitude is owed by all who love the Bible. As the church gained power and influence, especially during the third and fourth centuries, Jewish rabbis began to become concerned that the focus of attention was upon the "Christian" documents that were being widely distributed and copied.

Fearful that the Old Testament Scriptures would become corrupted or fall into disarray, pushed aside by more popular New Testament documents, two Jewish rabbinical schools were established, one in Caesarea on the Mediterranean and the other in Tiberias on Galilee. Their objective was to collect and organize the Old Testament documents, codify them, and preserve them. Little did they realize what a great service they were doing to the very church they feared, in that the Old Testament is the cradle of the New Testament. And though believers are under grace, not law, the Old Testament provides the foundation that brings understanding to the New.

Their contribution included:

- Adding vowels and accents to the text

- Developing a standard for pronunciation

- Collecting and classifying thousands of scrolls and documents

- Elevating respect for the Old Testament Scriptures

- Preserving authentic texts that became the standard for 1,500 years

On the margin of the text, the Masoretes would make annotations which were verifiable. Short of being able to access the entire text by a computer, it is inconceivable how a finer system could be put in place to ensure the accuracy of the transmission of Scripture.

The Bible Is Unique as the Official Biography of the World's Most Influential Person

Larry King, a popular television talk show host who interviewed many of the world's greats, never hesitated to ask tough questions, but on one occasion a guest turned the tables and asked him who he would most like to interview from a historical perspective. One of those he named was Jesus Christ.

"What would you have asked him?" the guest challenged him. The implications for Larry King, of course, were very weighty.

He replied, "I would like to ask him if he was indeed virgin born because the answer to that question would define history."[16] King, ethnically Jewish, went to the very heart of the issue—was Jesus' birth supernatural? If he was not born of a virgin, he was not who Scripture represents him to be, and he then would have been an impostor. Because the writers of the gospels present him as "born of a virgin" in fulfillment of prophecies, should he not have been virgin-born, everything else they wrote would be suspect. Was he the unique fulfillment of passages such as Isaiah 7:14 prophesying that the "virgin will conceive and give birth to a son"? The New Testament says he was, in clear and certain terms, with full understanding of the implications.

The central figure of the New Testament is Jesus Christ, and apart from the Bible, there is little to either instruct or inform us regarding his person, his mission, his life, death, and resurrection.

The New Testament is the official biography of this man, the most influential person in all history, the one whose coming became the Continental Divide of all history. While Jesus is mentioned by Josephus, the Jewish historian who became pro-Roman, as well as by Roman historians Tacitus and Suetonius, it is the twenty-seven books of the New Testament that flesh out the story.

Simply put, the New Testament documents demonstrate that Jesus was

- Unique in his birth and childhood

- Unique in his youth

- Unique in his ministry, starting about age 30

  ○ He said things no other person dared to say

  ○ He did things that cannot be explained apart from divinity

- Unique in suffering, death, and resurrection

C. S. Lewis sums it up well:

Either this man was, and is, the Son of God: or else a madman or something worse. You can shut him up for a fool, you can spit at him and kill him as a demon; or you can fall at his feet and call him Lord and God. But let us not come with any patronizing nonsense about his being a great human teacher. He has not left that open to us. He did not intend to.[17]

The Bible Is Unique in Its Message

The tremendous acceptance of Rick Warren's book *The Purpose Driven Life*—now with tens of millions of copies in print, having been on the *New York Times* bestseller list for more than forty-two consecutive months—is a reflection of the desire of people to know what life is about. The question of existence, what makes life meaningful, is one of the paramount issues of our day.

Prior to the publication of Warren's book, I was presented with a draft of the manuscript. Like other reviewers, I read the book and thought, "This is good and it will be helpful to a lot of people," but the book has been successful beyond anything that could be imagined. The phenomenal success of the book (even Pope John Paul II, it is reported, had a Polish copy of the book by his bedside at his death) is a reflection of the desire of people to fill the void and emptiness in their hearts.

Without elaboration I want to propose that the Bible alone answers the deep questions of life:

- Who am I?

- Where did I come from?

- Where do I go after I die?

- What is life about?

- Where is the world headed?

Those answers are found in no other book, no other source, or no other person, and that's what makes the Bible unique.

The Bottom Line

The Bible is unique. The planks of uniqueness are among the first you traverse as you cross the bridge of confidence in what the Bible says. You glimpse the fingerprints of the mighty hand of God in the timing, the manner, and the distinctive character of the book. And all of this leads to the next issue: the authenticity of the documents that comprise the Bible. That's why so much rests upon the primary evidence—the manuscripts and the stories they tell.

CHAPTER 2

THE POWERFUL TESTIMONY OF MANUSCRIPT EVIDENCE

*More than 5,750 manuscripts of the New Testament
exist today, making the New Testament the best-attested
document in all ancient writing.*
Norman L. Geisler[18]

You may be thinking, "What do a few old manuscripts have to do with my life today?" If you are concerned with the integrity of the Bible, they are of great importance. When very, very old manuscripts are discovered, and their substance is the same as the text of the Bible you have in your home or office, you are assured that the text has not been changed or altered; your confidence in what God tells you in the Bible increases.

God has providentially allowed the preservation of biblical manuscripts that have been passed from generation to generation. Realize also what a great contribution the science of biblical criticism has made to verifying and preserving the accuracy of the biblical text. This knowledge and understanding can carry you across the chasm of doubt or question.

It is more than coincidental that at the very time when science and technology seemed to eclipse spiritual values, God has seen it fit to allow manuscripts to be discovered that are at least 1,000 years older than anything of the same portion of Scripture in existence at the time of the discovery. Popular wisdom tells us that truth is always stranger than fiction. If you don't believe that, perhaps you will after you've read the following section.

The Remarkable Discoveries at Qumran

It was spring of 1947 and hostilities were escalating between Israel (not yet an independent nation) and her Arab neighbors. A young man, Jum'a Muhammed from the Ta'amireh Bedouin tribe, had lost some of the goats he was tending.[19] Muhammed began searching for them. Wandering up a wadi, or desolate valley, he saw a cave—something that was relatively common, caused by erosion when the rains gushed down the ravines towards the Dead Sea far below. "Is it possible that the goats may have wandered into the cave?" he thought.

He picked up a rock and threw it into the opening of the cave. The strange noise he heard, though, wasn't the bleating of a goat. "It's a spirit!" he thought, and fearful of what might be there, he tucked tail like a scared puppy and headed towards the warmth and security of the goat-skin tent which was the family home.

That evening, as the family sat around the fire recounting the events of the day, Muhammed told them how he had encountered an evil spirit. His cousins scoffed at him. "There's no such thing," they said, and to prove that, the next morning they accompanied their cousin to the cave to find out what had made the noise.

Reaching the cave high above the ravine was not easy, but they got there. And when they did, they discovered that the noise from the rock was the result of the stone's shattering an old earthenware vessel that originally was about thirty-six inches tall. Among the broken pieces of pottery they found an old scroll that centuries before had been placed in the jar and sealed with a kind of bituminous pitch—hardened by the hot, arid weather. The cousins were illiterate, so the writing on the scrolls meant nothing to them. Eight or nine other scrolls were in the cave, which came to be identified as Cave 1.

The story that I've just related is the popular one that I would like to believe, but may be a public relations sort of tale that makes good copy but embellishes what actually happened.[20]

Two days after the cave was initially discovered, one of the cousins (not Jum'a Muhammed, who originally located the cave but did not explore it) arose early in the morning while the other were sleeping and scaled the 350 or so feet to the cave's entrance, lowering himself feet first into the cave to see what treasure he might find.

Harry Thomas Frank describes what in all probability actually happened that day:

> At dawn of the next morning Muhammed Ahmed-el-Hamed, who was nicknamed "The Wolf" (edh-Dhib), woke first. Leaving his two cousins sleeping on the ground he scaled the 350 or so feet up to the cave.... With effort the slender young man was able to lower himself feet first into the cave. The floor was covered with debris including broken pottery. But along the wall stood a number of narrow jars, some with their bowl-shaped covers still in place. Edh-Dhib scrambled over the floor of the cave and plunged his hand into one of the jars. Nothing. Frantically he tore the cover from another, eagerly exploring the smooth inside of the empty container. Another and yet another with the same result. The ninth was full of dirt. The increasingly desperate young Bedouin at last closed his hand around something wrapped in cloth. He extracted two such bundles and then a third, which had a leather covering but no cloth wrapping. The cloth and the leather were greenish with age. These were all edh-Dhib took from the cave that morning.[21]

How the manuscript was discovered, however, does not affect the importance of what was found! Frank summarizes what happened this way: "Scholars who later interviewed edh-Dhib think that this boy had in his hands on that winter morning nothing less than the great Isaiah Scroll, the Habakkuk commentary, and the Manual of Discipline!"[22]

The cousins took the scrolls back to base camp. The Isaiah scroll was placed in a bag and hung on a tent pole for a period of time. Since Bedouins are nomadic, wandering from place to place searching for grass and water for their flocks, it was not until several weeks later that they went to Bethlehem, where they often traded with Khalil Iskander, a merchant who went by the name of Kando, and bartered the scroll for provisions and a small amount of money.

Did Kando know what he really had? Probably not at first, but he did have the savvy to realize any ancient scroll was worth some money (after all, he made his living hawking antiques and artifacts). Yes, he knew they were valuable, but how valuable they actually were never crossed his mind. When Kando first saw them, he thought they might be Syrian. He also knew he had "hot merchandise." Though Bethlehem was then in Jordanian hands, he knew that if authorities found out about the scrolls, they would immediately confiscate them and give him trouble. Big trouble. It is reported that to safeguard his cache for a period of time he buried the priceless 2,000-year-old scrolls behind his little shop.

By most accounts Kando originally bought three—possibly four—manuscripts from the Bedouins. Whether Kando then persuaded the Bedouins to return to the caves and search for more manuscripts or engaged in his own illicit excavations will never be known for certain. But the "battle for the scrolls" was on as Bedouins and archaeologists both searched the caves for contraband manuscripts.

Kando tried to determine what he really had and how valuable were the scrolls. He contacted a trusted friend, an Armenian living in the walled Old City of Jerusalem, who like himself dabbled in artifacts and antiques. The Armenian dealer made contact with Professor Eleazer Sukenik, who held the chair of Archaeology at Jerusalem's Hebrew University. The Armenian thought that Professor Sukenik might buy the scrolls for the university. By then it was almost a year later, and the 1948 War of Liberation had sealed Bethlehem from Israel proper. British authorities, then concerned with security issues, had erected barriers in the Old City, and to be allowed passage from one to the other required a military pass. Professor Sukenik agreed to meet the Armenian dealer the next morning. They had to see each other at the security terrace because the professor wanted to avoid being asked why he needed a pass. A "no-man's land" of hooped barbed wire separated the two men, and Sukenik watched with keen interest as enough of the scroll was unrolled for him to read some of the text.

I can only imagine his eyes focusing intently on the old Hebrew text as he recognized this was the book of Isaiah—and the oldest text he had ever seen. He later wrote in his journal that he had been "privileged by destiny to gaze upon a Hebrew scroll that had not been read for more than two thousand years."[23] Professor Sukenik, realizing the tremendous value of what he saw, arranged for the clandestine purchase of three of the scrolls. The remaining four scrolls were acquired by the Orthodox Archbishop Athanasius Yeshua Samuel, Metropolitan of the Syrian Jacobite Monastery of St. Mark in Jerusalem, who paid Kando twenty-four pounds, or about ninety-seven US dollars. The archbishop then sought to find out exactly what he had and how valuable they were.

It is at this point that a 33-year-old American, John Cecil Trever, became involved in the story. Trever graduated with honors from the University of Southern California with a degree in religion in 1937. The following year he married his sweetheart Elizabeth and then went to Yale where he took another undergraduate degree, then took two graduate degrees including a PhD in Old Testament with an emphasis on ancient Semitic languages and paleography (the study and analysis of ancient handwriting). Trever wrote his doctoral dissertation on the book of Isaiah, never thinking how important this research would ultimately become in his life.

Trever was also an amateur photographer who had an intense interest in microphotography and botany. In 1947, Trever was one of three men to receive a fellowship at the American School of Oriental Research in Jerusalem (now known as the Albright Institute of Archaeological Research). Before leaving for Israel, Trever took a crash course in developing color film, and Ansco (the film company that rivaled Eastman-Kodak at the time) gave Trever a trunk full of the latest equipment needed to develop the film. Packed with his gear was a new professional camera, one that he never thought would be used to show the world what had come out of the dark cave at Qumran.

Along with his equipment, Trever brought a newly acquired set of thirty-five millimeter slides of the Nash Papyri[24] and had become sufficiently familiar with them to recognize the similarities in style and structure with the Isaiah manuscript. He first saw the manuscript on February 20, 1948 when Archbishop Samuel and two of his fellow monks came to the institute bearing the scrolls they had acquired.

Trever and his colleague William Brownlee immediately identified the text from Isaiah, the Old Testament book that had been the subject of Trever's doctoral research. After he convinced the archbishop that he was trustworthy—not a small accomplishment, as he related in correspondence to his wife—the archbishop agreed to leave the scrolls with him overnight. According to his wife, Trever immediately began photographing the manuscript, working all night because of the uncertainty as to how long he would be allowed to keep them.[25]

With the archbishop's permission, Trever sent the prints to Professor William Foxwell Albright, his friend and mentor at the American school of Oriental Research at Johns Hopkins, who was recognized as the dean of biblical paleographic and archaeological research. Albright, probably the most widely-recognized authority of manuscript dating, established the accepted date that the scroll was produced at around 100 BC. "The quality of his photographs often exceeded that of the scrolls themselves over the years, as the texts quickly eroded once removed from their linen wraps," says an observer.[26]

Was John Trever in Jerusalem by chance or was he part of God's greater plan? Did God prepare him to be at the right spot at the exact time with his unusual qualifications, including a doctoral dissertation that allowed him to recognize the importance of what he saw? That was the question I asked Trever's wife, Elizabeth, much later. She affirmed the latter in no uncertain terms. Almost daily Trever wrote to her as he shared his excitement and joy at being able to help identify documents that had been buried for some 1,900 years in a dark cave.

The following year, Archbishop Samuel took the scrolls to New York, seeking to sell them for the greatest possible amount. Thereafter, the scrolls seemed to fade from the radar screen.

Now, fast forward some five years. On June 1, 1954, an advertisement appeared in the *Wall Street Journal* captioned, "Four Dead Sea Scrolls for Sale." Here is the rest of the story:

> The advertisement was brought to the attention of Yigael Yadin, Professor Sukenik's son, who had just retired as chief of staff of the Israel Defense Forces and had reverted to his primary vocation, archaeology. With the aid of intermediaries, the four scrolls were purchased from Mar Samuel for $250,000. Thus, the scrolls that had eluded Yadin's father because of the war were now at his disposal. Part of the purchase price was contributed by D. S. Gottesman, a New York philanthropist. His heirs sponsored construction of the Shrine of the Book in Jerusalem's Israel Museum, in which these unique manuscripts are exhibited to the public.[27]

How old is the scroll of Isaiah, a replica of which you will find as a centerpiece of the Shrine of the Book in Jerusalem? Before the discovery of the Isaiah manuscript, the oldest Hebrew text of Isaiah was a manuscript in book form known as a codex. Since it was found near Cairo, Egypt, it was dubbed the Cairo Codex. It contains the Old Testament prophetic books and is dated AD 895. So, the newly discovered text of Isaiah pushes back the age for an existent manuscript of the book of Isaiah by about 1,000 years.

If the text of Scripture has been altered, amended, or tampered with as some claim (such as the publications whose featured titles I quoted at the beginning of the chapter), it would readily become apparent as the Isaiah manuscript found at Qumran is laid side by side and compared with the manuscript dated AD 895.

What has changed in the Isaiah text? Nothing of substance, say scholars. The variations are slight—obvious slips of the pen and misspelling, differences in structure—but nothing that is significant—a remarkable testimony to the integrity of the Scriptures. Two of the Isaiah scrolls found in the Qumran trove are "word for word identical" with the traditional Masoretic text.[28]

The scrolls that came out of Cave 1 were the first to attract notoriety; however, since 1947, no stone has been left unturned. Some forty caves have given up over 800 documents, including portions of every Old Testament book in the Bible with the exception of the book of Esther. Without exception, those important manuscripts and documents have only substantiated the text of our Bible;

several of those manuscripts, however, add additional light to the history of biblical times and the structure of the New Testament books.

Sir Frederick Kenyon, former director of the British Museum and author of *The Palaeography of Greek Papyri,* writes, "In no other case is the interval of time between the composition of the book and the date of the earliest manuscript so short as in that of the New Testament."[29] In his book *The Bible and Archaeology* he says, "The last foundation for any doubt that the Scriptures have come down to us substantially as they were written has now been removed."[30] The following is part of the evidence supporting Kenyon's position.

The Remarkable Journey of an Old Scroll from St. Catherine's to the British Library

Around AD 550, the Emperor Justinian built the fortress that is St. Catherine's Monastery on a narrow gorge in the Sinai Peninsula to protect monks from the raiding Saracen tribes. It was believed that this was where God spoke to Moses through the burning bush.

Reaching St. Catherine's today is quite difficult, but in the 1840s, when a twenty-nine-year-old man came to the world's oldest monastery, it was far more challenging. The young man's name was Constantin von Tischendorf. One of the nineteenth century's most brilliant and colorful scholars, Tischendorf in all probability is owed a greater debt than any other person when it comes to preserving and illuminating biblical manuscripts. During his lifetime, this German-born son of a physician logged more miles on the back of horses and camels, in carriages, and by ship than a lot of platinum club world travelers today.

In his book *How We Got the Bible*, Neil Lightfoot tells how the young, brash Tischendorf arrived by camel caravan at St. Catherine's in 1844. After he presented his credentials, he was hoisted by monks over the door—a thirty-foot-high barricade that remained closed for security purposes—on a crossbar. His was not a religious pilgrimage, but a scholar's search for biblical documents. Throughout his life, Tischendorf remained committed to the premise that he was seeking neither fame nor financial rewards, but to eliminate questions regarding the text of the Bible.

Several years earlier, Tischendorf earned hash marks of academic credentials with the publication of a critical edition of the Greek Testament. He was serious, brilliant, motivated, and daring. He was given a small apartment at the monastery and undoubtedly scrutinized by the aged monks, who were not quite certain what to do with this highly acclaimed young man.

One morning Tischendorf noticed that the librarian was lighting a fire using old sheets of parchment. He noticed that among them were "a considerable number of sheets of a copy of the Old Testament in Greek" that, according to Tischendorf, were "the most ancient that I had ever seen."[31]

Several basketsful of these ancient pieces of parchment had already been fed to the fire; however, he was able to acquire about forty-three of these pages—one-third of the pile—and upon his return to his home in Leipzig he published them, telling no one where he had found them.

Wanting to get the rest of them, he returned to St. Catherine's in 1853, where to his great disappointment no one seemed to know anything about the remaining sheets of parchment. Had they been burned? Were they holding out on him? Had someone else visited there, paid a "king's ransom" for the lot, and packed them off somewhere else? He wasn't sure. He did, however, observe that part of one was being used for a bookmark. He recognized it as coming from Genesis 24, leading him to be relatively certain that the original scroll had to include the entire Old Testament in Greek (known as the Septuagint).

Months turned into years. Tischendorf was getting older, yet he was still determined to make one more trip to St. Catherine's. Thus in 1859 under the sponsorship of Alexander II, the Czar of Russia, he made the long, weary trip down into the Negev to the monastery.

Again, nothing! No one talked. No one seemed to know anything. Disappointed, he gave up and advised his Bedouin couriers to prepare to leave within three days. In the afternoon, however, the steward of the monastery invited him to have tea with him in his cloister that evening. Upon arriving at his room, the steward said, "And I, too, have read a Septuagint," and produced what Tischendorf later described as "a bulky kind of volume, wrapped in a red cloth."

Although he was ecstatic, this time he masked his excitement, fearing that the youthful exuberance he had displayed fifteen years earlier had left the impression that they had something extremely valuable that, like gold, should be kept in a safe-deposit vault. He asked permission, however, to take the scroll to his room overnight.

He described his elation, saying,

> I knew that I held in my hand the most precious biblical treasure in existence—a document whose age and importance exceeded that of all the manuscripts which I had ever examined during twenty years' study of the subject. I cannot now, I confess, recall all the emotions which I felt in that exciting moment with such a diamond in my possession.[32]

"The first thing he did when he reached his room," writes Dr. Ludwig Schneller, in a biography of his famous father-in-law, "was to go down on his knees and thank God for the nearly miraculous find."[33]

Tischendorf convinced the monks that the manuscript could better be studied in Cairo and arranged to take it there, returning it at a later time. The manuscript, known today as the Sinai Manuscript, never found its way back to the old monastery. It was taken to Russia and shown to the czar, who, if you remember, had financed the expedition. After much haggling and disagreement among the monks, the manuscript was officially given to the Russian czar in exchange for 9,000 Russian rubles and medals. It remained in St. Petersburg long after the czar died, but in 1933 when the nearly bankrupt communist government needed money, it was sold to the British museum for the sum of £100,000 (then about the sum of $500,000).

An interesting sidebar regarding the sum of money that was paid, which in 1933 represented a considerable fortune, is the fact that the same day the transaction took place, a first edition of the works by François-Marie Arouet de Voltaire was sold in a flea market in Paris for the equivalent sum of eleven cents in US currency. And who was Voltaire? A nineteenth-century intellectual and philosopher who is most remembered by Christians as the man who said Christianity would not survive him by 100 years.[34]

I shall never forget my first visit to the British Museum, walking through the corridor where the Sinai Manuscript was prominently displayed (it has since been moved and is now housed at the British Library). When I saw the manuscript for the first time, I was filled with awe and wonder. It was not the same kind of wonder that

I would experience when I see a sunset over the ocean or hold a newborn infant in my arms, but the kind that is the result of knowing that over the centuries God providentially allowed something to survive the ravages of time and decay.

Apart from the sentiment, how is the Sinai Manuscript important and what does it contribute to our confidence that the Bible is the Word of God?

First, with the exception of missing fragments of the text, this document is generally considered to be the oldest, complete manuscript of the entire Bible.[35] Dated by scholars at about AD 350, the Sinai Manuscript establishes a benchmark of comparison and contributes to our knowledge and understanding of what has happened in the intervening centuries.[36] Along with Vatican Codex, the Sinai Manuscript is recognized as one of the two finest manuscripts of the Bible in existence.

Another Hidden Pearl of Great Price

It is both ironic and chagrining that the most important biblical manuscript, both in completeness and accuracy, lay hidden in a nondescript repository in the Vatican for years before the world of scholarship had access to it.

Dated at about AD 325, the Vatican Codex found its way to Rome and the Vatican sometime in the fifteenth century. It lay there, preserved and silent, until—you guessed it—Constantin von Tischendorf appeared on the scene. Having learned of its strategic importance, Tischendorf petitioned the Vatican to see it. The Vatican reluctantly gave him permission to examine the text, with one caveat: he was not allowed to copy a single line of the text.

Undeterred, this bold and brilliant scholar, whose IQ must have been pushing genius levels, would memorize the text each brief period he was permitted to view the manuscript. At night in the privacy of his room he would painstakingly write down verbatim what he had seen, letter by letter, sentence by sentence.

Then the crisis came. Unable to restrain himself one day, he jotted down a few sentences on paper so he could compare it with the text found at Mt. Sinai. He was caught in the act of scribbling by an observant librarian and denied any further access to this precious document.

The Story a Document Tells

Without question, every manuscript has a story to tell. A scholar doesn't need to have a background in criminal investigation to know what it is, but there are markers that are important. One such marker is the kind of material the scroll is written on. Largely because of the expense and the unavailability of more durable writing substances, most biblical manuscripts have been written on papyrus, the forerunner of paper as we know it. The problem with papyrus is that it doesn't hold up indefinitely since it is made of organic matter. And that is precisely why we don't have the original manuscripts—the ones written by the writers of the various books themselves.

Better is parchment or vellum (a high-grade quality of parchment made of the skins of young animals) because this endures indefinitely. The best quality writing material was calfskin, coming from an unborn or a stillborn calf. But the problem here is that each page required a piece of hide that had been scraped and prepared to take ink. It was both expensive and time-consuming, to say nothing of the fact it was not nearly as readily available as papyri sheets.[37]

Generally the following guidelines are noted:

- Papyri – first to fourth century
- Parchment – fourth to eighth century
- Vellum (skins of antelope or calves) – eighth to fourteenth century

Another detail that was important was the kind of ink used. Why is this important? Because the kind of ink, the handwriting style, and the composition of the same were often tell-tale markers revealing when and where the manuscript was written. Every ancient document adds to our knowledge of this marvelous book we call the Bible.

How Did We End Up with What We Call "the Bible" Today?

The following discussion is not a definitive answer to that question. However, it gives you a brief summary of how the sixty-six books you find in your Bible came to be recognized as authoritative.

In most English Bibles, you will find thirty-nine books in the Old Testament and twenty-seven in the New Testament. But how do we know these are "the only ones" that are authoritative and belong in the Bible? What about more recent discoveries including some of the scrolls and writings found in the Caves of Qumran?

Let's start with the thirty-nine Old Testament books, which were written over a period of about 1,000 years. The selection of the books forming the Old Testament, according to the knowledge we have today, was never problematic—questioned and challenged, yes, but never in jeopardy. Hundreds of times, writers invoked the Almighty as their source of authority by saying, "Thus says the Lord," a powerful, almost indisputable certification to uniqueness.

Moses wrote the books of the law known as the Pentateuch. Following the conquest of Canaan, Joshua's book telling of the conquest was added to the collection, which stayed intact until there was a final home for them in Jerusalem.

From Joshua's day to the time of Solomon, prophets, priests, and poets recorded history and wisdom literature. When the temple was completed under Solomon, these books, along with some prophetic writings, were considered to be sacred and authoritative, and were eventually preserved. Daniel referred to this collection as "the Scriptures" (Daniel 9:2), and Isaiah called them "the scroll of the LORD" (Isaiah 34:16). The writings of Isaiah, Jeremiah, and Daniel (considered to be major prophetic books because of their length) were then added to this collection along with fourteen final prophetic books, Hosea through Malachi (referred to as minor prophetic books because of their shorter length).

During the days of Ezra and Nehemiah, following the Babylonian captivity, the Old Testament books as we know them today were essentially codified and recognized by all Jews, bringing the Old Testament canon to completion about 432 BC.

Were there other religious books in existence? Yes, there were—probably many of them, now lost to posterity. Joshua 10:13 and 2 Samuel 1:18 both refer to the Book of Jashar. But there was a consensus as to what was God-given and to be accepted and revered and what was interesting but did not possess the sense of divine urgency and stamp of the Almighty.

It was the church, however, that was confronted with the task of determining what books are unquestionably inspired by the Holy Spirit and should be included in the New Testament, and what books are perhaps factual and even offer spiritual comfort and encouragement but lack the same ring of authority as do other books. Now, let's go to the issues surrounding the New Testament starting with the first four books.

Today, we commonly refer to those first four books in the New Testament as the gospels; however, the early church referred to these four simply as "the gospel," not considering each one "a gospel."

The gospels, it is generally agreed, came together very quickly and were accepted as Scripture after John wrote the book that bears his name. The New Testament letters, however, were another matter. Of the twenty-one letters in the New Testament, thirteen came from the pen of the Apostle Paul. They were arranged by length, with the longest book, Romans, being placed first in the group and Philemon, the shortest, concluding the group of letters.

Paul, however, wrote far more letters than those included in the New Testament. For instance, we know for a fact that he wrote at least four letters to the church at Corinth. In his first letter, he reminds them that in his previous letter, he told them "not to associate with sexually immoral people" (1 Corinthians 5:9); and in 2 Corinthians 10 Paul alludes to previous letters addressing problems in the church. Today, we have only two of Paul's letters to Corinth. It is only logical that Paul, following the pattern of ministering to a church, then addressing the needs of that group by letter after he left them, would have written many more letters than we have now in the Bible. Of note is the fact that Paul asserted that what he wrote had been inspired or directed by God himself.[38]

We also know that individual letters to specific churches were read in other churches, someone removing the name of the recipient and replacing it with the name of the secondary church. "After this letter has been read to you," Paul wrote to the Colossians, "see that it is also read in the church of the Laodiceans and that you in turn read the letter from Laodicea" (Colossians 4:16).

Peter acknowledged Paul's unique authority saying he wrote with "the wisdom that God gave him," recognizing that some things written by Paul "are hard to understand," yet put them in the same category as "other Scriptures" (2 Peter 3:15–16).

The other eight letters known as general letters include Hebrews, James, 1 and 2 Peter, the three letters of John, and Jude. A number of these letters were somewhat controversial, subjected to differing opinions as to whether they were, in fact, inspired by the Holy Spirit and should be universally accepted by believers everywhere. Why the controversy? Part of the answer is the lack of communication between individuals who were separated by geography and lacked the facility of dialogue as we know today. Neil Lightfoot explains,

> Because these collections were made at different times and places, the contents of the various collections were not always the same. This helps to explain why not all of the New Testament books were at first received without hesitation; while in other instances uncertainty of a book's authorship, as in the case of Hebrews, presented temporary obstacles to universal acceptance.[39]

The Bottom Line

The Bible is the best preserved and best documented book in the world. In 1972 the late renowned scholar Dr. Charles Ryrie wrote, "More than 5,000 manuscripts of the New Testament exist today which makes the New Testament the best-attested document in all ancient writing." Today, however, that number has increased to over 5,750 manuscripts—the result of archaeological finds throughout the Middle East. That number swells when we include the more than 86,000 quotes of the New Testament found in the sermons and writings of the early church fathers, along with translations into Latin, Aramaic, and other languages of the first to the fifth centuries.

Church historian Dr. Edward Panosian says that all of the passages or words about which there is even the slightest question would be no more than a half-page of a 500-page book. That doesn't leave much room for conjecture. And I have to add that no single doctrinal issue is questioned—none.

Totally without foundation is the myth that the Bible has been copied and recopied, translated and retranslated so that today what we have doesn't even resemble the original as written by Moses, the prophets, Mathew, Mark, Luke, and John, along with the apostle Paul and other writers. Those who allege this demonstrate their ignorance of the facts.

Whether or not you use the book as a measure of truth, a guide for your life, and a blueprint for living, the evidence supporting its veracity and integrity is overwhelming. It cannot be ignored.

THE CONTRIBUTION OF ARCHAEOLOGY

No archaeological discovery has ever controverted a biblical reference.
Nelson Glueck,[40] Jewish archaeologist

What Is Modern Archaeology About?

Let's begin with a working definition of archaeology as "the scientific study of the remains of the past." The English word "archaeology" comes from two Greek words, αρχιος and λογος, and literally means "the study of ancient things." In a broad sense, it can be considered the scientific study of people, cultures, and civilizations which have been lost and recovered through a variety of disciplines and means.

Naturally this gives rise to the question, "How did cities as well as nations such as the Hittites get 'lost' anyway?" Some cities, such as Nineveh, had so completely disappeared that the army of Alexander the Great marched by and didn't even know that they were passing the ruins of a once-great city. Much later, Napoleon Bonaparte and his army passed by the ancient city of Babylon and never knew it was there either.

Obviously, some landmarks have not disappeared. The pyramids, built as early as 1,000 years before Moses, are relatively permanent. They have stood the test of time and are expected to continue standing for many, many years. Geographic landmarks such as Galilee, the Valley of Esdralon where Armageddon will take place, Elisha's fountain at Jericho, the vast fortress of Masada where 960 patriots took their lives rather than surrender to the Romans in AD 73, Mt. Hermon, the Kidron Valley, and the Mount of Olives, will remain very much as they are even at the present time. But other landmarks, nations, and significant structures had all but vanished until they were resurrected by modern archaeology. Questions such as "Why did they disappear?" and "What happened?" are valid.

Modern archaeology takes away the conjecture and offers explanations as to what happened to nations and people as well as cities and places. It shows how a city may have been built in a certain location because it had an accessible water supply, or the site was readily defensible, or it was located on a trade route or harbor, ensuring economic viability. Then hostility with a neighboring nation or people resulted in its destruction. After the war, the buildings—having been constructed mostly of mud brick with little reinforcement—were leveled, and a new city was built on the ruins of the old, thus burying the previous level and everything in it.

At times famine or drought drove people away. A harbor silted over a period of several centuries and eventually the livelihood from shipping became diminished to the point that people moved away. Such happened to the great city of Ephesus, where the Cayster River flowed into the Aegean Sea. Today, the old coastline is some five miles inland, whereas in Paul's day Ephesus was a harbor.

Earthquakes also took their toll on cities. Locals, thinking that the quake was the act of a god, would not rebuild on the same site. And so the rubble and sand began to pile up, about a foot a century, and eventually the place would be marked by a mound known as a tell. Nobody, of course, bothered to put up a sign saying, "Here lies the ruins of ancient (fill in the blank)," and with the passing of generations, details about these places were replaced by legends.

Other cities were destroyed and not rebuilt because of the judgment of God. The great city of Tyre was destroyed and not reconstructed, just as the prophet Ezekiel foretold, because of the manner in which they had mocked Israel (see Ezekiel 26:2–3). Likewise, according to the eighth-century prophet Obadiah, the Edomites were driven out of the red city of Petra for the same reason.

It is little wonder that archaeology has always been cloaked with fascination as well as mystique as to what hidden treasure could be found—whether it was gold in an Egyptian tomb that had been sealed for 3,000 years or an ossuary (stone box) with an inscription on the side of it bearing a secret code.

"Biblical archaeology has changed drastically from 100 years ago, when its focus was on treasure hunting and finding artifacts to 'prove the Bible true,'" says writer Jeffery Sheler.[41] He's right. The days of the simple dig-and-discover method are long gone. Scientific knowledge and the tools of technology have greatly changed the way archaeologists ply their skills.

While archaeology is not an exact science like chemistry or mathematics with their formulas and precepts, it has developed into a fairly complex discipline involving many different facets of exploration and analysis. Today an archaeologist is now like a general practitioner in medicine who, as necessity dictates, calls in specialists to deal with areas where he lacks expertise. He may call upon chemists, hematologists, geologists, climatologists, anthropologists, DNA experts, computer specialists, and forensic experts. Today even satellite imaging and radar get into the act.

Modern archaeology began in 1799 when the forces of Napoleon Bonaparte discovered the Rosetta Stone during Napoleon's French incursion into Egypt. Soldiers were digging the foundation of an addition to a fort near the town of el-Rashid (Rosetta) and one of the soldiers in the expedition by the name of Boussard found a huge slab of black granite. When the spade struck the rock, little did he know or even imagine what a vast treasure he was about to uncover.

The black slab measured 45 inches by 28 ½ inches, 11 inches thick. Written on this stele are three languages—fourteen lines of Egyptian hieroglyphics, thirty-two lines of demotic, and fifty-four lines of Greek in large letters known as uncials. It was nearly a century later, in 1882, that a French scholar, Jean François Champollion, deciphered the writing.

When the French lost the war, the English expropriated the treasure and carted it off to the British Museum in 1802, where it has remained except for two years when it was securely ensconced in a London subway fifty feet below ground so that it would be safe from the devastation of German bombs in World War II.

What Do Archaeological Expeditions Find?

Archaeological expeditions uncover the same kind of things that you have in your house—ordinary items that relate to your life and culture. The difference is that what was considered ordinary about 3,000 years ago may be considered extraordinary today.

A stroll through almost any museum reveals an abundance of things such as clothing, cooking utensils, pottery of all sizes, shapes, and descriptions (often a key to providing dates), knives, weapons, coins, human remains, statues of all sizes (for example, the largest building in ancient Ephesus, adjacent to the city hall, has been identified as a house of prostitution by the artifacts thrown into a well), letters and notes (usually written on papyrus), and so forth.

What Does Archaeology Contribute to Biblical Understanding?

1. Archaeology has confirmed the names of literally thousands of geographic places, such as Bethlehem, Caesarea, Rome, Ephesus, Laodicea, Nineveh, Babylon, Tyre, Sidon, Dan, Beersheba, the House of Caiaphas, Corinth (including the meat market and the bema or judgment seat where Paul refuted false charges), and the synagogue in Capernaum.

2. Archaeology demonstrates that individuals such as Abraham and Sarah, Moses, David, Pilate, and a great number of kings—of Israel and Judah as well as those of other kingdoms—once lived and reigned or otherwise influenced history.[42] The extensive findings at Mari, in Syria, refuted the beliefs of some scholars who taught that writing hadn't even been formulated during the time

when Moses wrote the Pentateuch. Thousands of tablets found here demonstrate that names such as those of the patriarchs Abraham, Isaac, and Jacob, as well as many other names mentioned in Scripture, were commonly used during the era the Bible speaks of.

3. Archaeology helps us understand events mentioned in Scripture in light of the cultures in which they took place. Remember Ephron, the Hittite? Abraham needed a place to bury Sarah at her death and was interested in buying the cave at Machpelah from his neighbor. Ephron said, "It's yours—my gift to you!" But he really didn't mean that. It was the culture, we have learned—part of the bargaining process. Finally he said, "The land is worth four hundred shekels of silver," and the deal was struck (Genesis 23:15). God made covenants with his people which follow the same pattern of covenants and legal documents of the times.

4. Archaeology has resulted in a vast number of manuscript discoveries (the papyri are among the finest examples of this) giving us insights to culture, the meaning of words, the vagaries of human nature and the customs of people, confirming the data found in the Bible. For

example, in October, 1967, four months after the Six-Day War, Israeli archaeologists exploring Masada found scrolls that had been buried there for 2,000 years amidst the ruins. Says Moshe Perlman, speaking of a manuscript containing the Psalms that was found there, "The Psalms of David as recited in today's synagogues are the same as those uttered by the Zealots in their synagogues—the same Hebrew words, the same sentence structure, the same beginning and end of each chapter."

5. Archaeological findings that make biblical places and events come alive in that geography are the hook on which history is hung. The more we know of the actual environment and climate, the greater is our understanding of certain events mentioned in Scripture, such as floods, drought, earthquakes, and disasters.

6. Archaeology has shed much light on the language of Scripture. For instance, Peter told his readers to "Make every effort to confirm your calling and election" (2 Peter 1:10). The word "confirm," archaeologist have discovered, was used in legal documents of the Roman era. In a contract it meant the stipulations could not be changed. In a will, it meant that heirs could not alter the terms

of the testament. Found in a love letter, the suitor assured his beloved that he would always love her. "Make every effort to confirm your calling and election" takes on new meaning in light of this discovery about the word use of "confirm."

7. Finally, archaeology provides a window to the peoples mentioned in the Bible—a very lucid and meaningful one, too, that makes them come alive even in the twenty-first century. The Bible was not written in a vacuum but in our world: a world of flesh and blood, of commerce, of intrigue, of love and death; and the more archaeologists have unearthed, the greater is our understanding of the times in which the Word was given and the people to whom it was given. No place on earth has been more excavated than Israel, the crossroads of civilization and the birthplace of Judaism and Christianity.

The limited space in this book does not allow an exhaustive study of important archaeological discoveries of the past century. I have, however, singled out five representative stories that demonstrate that archaeology is a solid bridge to confidence in God's Word.

EXHIBIT 1: Landsat Does Its Stuff

Satellite imagery, which was first developed with military objectives in mind, became a new tool for archaeologists who wanted to pin down the locations of long-forgotten cities—at least, forgotten to the thousands of people who thumb through the pages of their Old Testament and stumble over words like Beersheba, Zer Hammoth, Abel Beth-Maacah, Napthali, and Tirzah. But some 4,000 years ago, these places were as meaningful to people as Manila, Frankfurt, Tokyo, or New York.

When Landsat began sending back pictures from space, scientists began seeing the faces of the earth in a new light. It was almost as if someone had switched on the light and enabled them to see ancient trade routes in the Middle East, which archaeologists knew were somewhere "out there," but now precisely became "down there."

In ancient days, when a city was destroyed in warfare, the survivors were usually taken away as slaves and the city was sacked and burned. Unlike the cities destroyed in World War II, which were rebuilt, the wind and sand began to drift over these ancient cities and they were soon lost to history. Satellite imaging makes these stand out vividly and enables scientists to chart transportation routes and identify undiscovered landmarks.

Archaeologists are making some remarkable discoveries which should only enhance our trust in the historical accuracy of the Bible. You may wonder, "Like what?" For a start, the exodus of some 2.5 million slaves from Egypt to the promised land of Canaan was one of the greatest migrations ever undertaken by a nation. Can archaeologists help document this move?

According to the Bible, Moses led the group in a rather circuitous path, avoiding the immediate and direct route from the Nile River delta where they were living in to Canaan. People sometimes quip that Moses was lost for forty years because he didn't want to stop and ask directions. Don't you believe that for a moment.

Jeffery Sheler explains,

> Recent archaeological data, scholars note, also are consistent with the Bible's explanation, in Exodus 13:17, about why Moses and the Israelites took the long way to Canaan through the desolate Sinai wilderness rather than following the shorter coastal route: Enemy military posts lay on that path. Egyptian hieroglyphics from about 1300 BC at the temple of Amun in Karnak depict a series of Egyptian installations along the coastal route. And modern excavations have uncovered a string of Egyptian citadels strikingly similar to those in the Karnak relief, stretching from the Nile delta to Gaza.[43]

Archaeologists from The Hebrew University of Jerusalem agree. The presence of the forts "is perfectly compatible with the Exodus," says Professor Trude Dothan. At the same time, archaeologists don't expect to find parking meters and leftover parts from their wagons. These who came out of Egypt were slaves and traveled light. Much like the Bedouins who still trek across the Negev, their tracks being erased by the wind and sand with not much left behind.

Score one for modern technology.

EXHIBIT 2: Discoveries at En Hatzeva

An old fortress some twenty miles southwest of the Dead Sea in Israel today has been called "one of the most spectacular finds of recent decades in all Israel." Today, archaeologists are unearthing the walls of a massive Iron Age fortress built about 800 BC, which is about 300 feet on each side and had massive towers on each corner. "OK," you may be thinking, "but why get worked up over a pile of very old rocks in a desert?" That is a good question. And the answer goes deeper than archaeology. It embraces the historical trustworthiness of the Bible at the same time.

Historians got excited when the old fortress was clearly identified as that which belonged to one of ancient Israel's most bitter enemies. Archaeologists got animated when they discovered an old Edomite shrine with some sixty-seven bowls with cultic images on them. Scholars of the Bible got excited because they recalled the prophecies of both Isaiah and Obadiah—two prophets of the eighth century who predicted that Edom and its power would be absolutely smashed to pieces. I get excited when I see another instance when the spade of the archaeologist confirms the historical record, reminding us that what is found in this book is authentic.

Among the ruins at En Hatzeva, where the fortress and the cultic shrine are located, were found seven large limestone incense altars decorated with human-like figures. The artifacts that archaeologists found had all been placed in a pit and smashed to pieces, obviously by someone who wanted to destroy them entirely. Imagine their amazement if those who stomped them so thoroughly could see them today, some 2,500 to 2,800 years later, reconstructed painstakingly by archaeologists.

Historians are surprised to find something belonging to the Edomites within territory which belonged to the kingdom of Judah, for En Hatzeva is located not in Edom but in Israel. Travelers to the Middle East today identify the rosy red city of Petra as the home of the ancient Edomites, but Petra, in Jordan today, is a long way from En Hatzeva, which seemingly proves that the Edomites had extended their influence and power far into territory belonging to Israel.

There are many unanswered questions, but we do know two things: First—the very presence of the Edomites was abhorrent to Judah. Edomites had on at least three occasions refused to let Israel pass through their territory when they came into the Promised Land. This had never been forgotten. Then, the gods of the Edomites, including their images and deities, were repulsive to Israel. The first of the Ten Commandments God gave to Moses forbade the worship of any other god, and the second restricted making any images.

How does all this relate to our lives today? The Scripture in 2 Kings 23 tells how King Josiah destroyed the idols of the Sidonians, Ammonites, and Moabites. What archaeologists have found may well be part of that massive cleansing of pagan worship. It also tells us that the prophecies about Edom were fulfilled, literally and precisely.

If what archaeologists have found gives you greater confidence as you pick up your Bible and read, then all the better. God's timetable is different from ours, yet what he says—whether it be of individuals, nations, or the world—will eventually take place. With that confidence Isaiah wrote, "Grass dries up, and flowers wither when the LORD's breath blows on them. Yes, people are like grass. Grass dries up, and flowers wither, but our God's word will last forever" (Isaiah 40:7–8, GW).

EXHIBIT 3: The Walls of Old Jericho

Could an earthquake have destroyed ancient Jericho at precisely the exact moment when Joshua and the warriors of ancient Israel marched around the walls seven times and then blew their trumpets? Amos Nur, a Stanford University geophysicist who has been studying the 10,000-year-long historical record of earthquakes in the Jordan Valley, thinks so. He says that Jericho "sits practically on the Jordan Fault that divides the Arabian plate from the Sinai plate."

National Geographic magazine quotes the scientist who notes that the walls of Jericho collapsed in a single direction, as they would in an earthquake, not in a variety of directions as they would if they were destroyed by an invading army.[44]

Many people presume it was Joshua's army that destroyed the walls of Jericho. But read the record: "When the trumpets sounded, the army shouted, and at the sound of the trumpet, when the men gave a loud shout, the wall collapsed; so everyone charged straight in, and they took the city" (Joshua 6:20). Even a casual reading makes it clear that it was God, not the army or psychological warfare, that destroyed ancient Jericho. Could God have used an earthquake? There is nothing that would eliminate that possibility.

Actually, Amos Nur, the scientist I quoted, wasn't the first to suggest than an earthquake may have been physical cause of the wall's collapse. Dr. John Garstang, director of the British School of Archaeology in Jerusalem, excavated Jericho between 1929 and 1936. Garstang found that the walls did actually "fall down flat" (using his terminology).[45] Garstang also noted that the walls fell outward and dragged the inner walls and houses with it, as would take place in an earthquake. Garstang contended that fire destroyed the existing grain supplies and the remains of the city, evidence that chaos resulted from this cataclysmic disturbance.

Geologists tell us that the Jordan Valley is like a giant split in a sandwich. It separates the Arabian Desert (which we know as Jordan, Iran and Iraq today) from the gentle hills adjacent to the Mediterranean. Starting from Galilee, at an altitude of 700 feet below sea level, the Jordan River Valley drops to 1,300 feet below sea level at the Dead Sea. A giant seismic fault runs deep through that valley.

The theory that God may have used an earthquake seems to be rational, yet it doesn't, for a moment, remove God from the landscape of human history. We then are faced with a miracle of timing that defies human explanation. Even today, nobody knows when an earthquake is going to take place. We only know when it happens. Apart from a supernatural revelation of God, anyone who positions himself around the walls of a city and blows his trumpet expecting an earthquake would be considered deranged and a candidate for an institution.

God normally uses the natural laws, which he puts into operation in a supernatural manner, to do his bidding. Amos Nur may well be right.

Subsequent to the excavations of John Garstang in the 1930s, another archaeologist, a fellow Briton by the name of Kathleen Kenyon, excavated again, taking exception with Garstang's findings. Her verdict: "No, that's not how it was at all. Wrong dates." While the jury is still out, she did find something fascinating.

She discovered that at the time of Christ, there were at least two sections of Jericho—an old part, and a newer part where the city wall had been extended, much as we would extend the city limits today to accommodate growth. Her findings reconciled what had appeared to be a conflict in Scripture. Because walls provided protection from enemies and defined city boundaries, a second wall was erected around the perimeters of the "newer" Jericho.

The text of Mark says that on a certain occasion Jesus was leaving Jericho when he encountered a blind man by the name of Bartimaeus, who cried out for help[46] (Mark 10:46–47), and Luke says he was going into the city (Luke 18:35). It appeared to be a contradiction—that's what skeptics said for a long while. True, it's difficult to be going into a city at the same time you are departing from one. How does archaeology help us reconcile this apparent contradiction?

Kenyon's excavations have shown that as Jericho grew, an annexation prior to the time of Christ had taken place—a kind of suburban Jericho in the terminology of our day. Bartimaeus may have been blind but he wasn't dumb. He knew that sitting at the gate or passageway between these two areas would be a place of high traffic and more people would notice him. His chances of getting more alms were better. Thus, the conflict between the writers is resolved. Jesus was passing out of one part of Jericho and into the other when he encountered Bartimaeus. Score another one for archaeology.

EXHIBIT 4: Jezebel's Makeup

An archaeological expedition digging at the site of ancient Samaria struck it rich—no, not gold! When it became clear that the ivory palace of Ahab and Jezebel had been identified, excitement filled the camp. In the queen's chambers of the palace of the ancient monarch were the very saucers and small stone boxes which Jezebel had used in mixing her cosmetics. It was all there, having been preserved despite the destruction of the palace. Traces of coal had been used for black; turquoise for green; ocher for red, and a small, smooth depression in the stone box was used for mixing the eye shadow.

Jezebel was one of the most powerful and ruthless people mentioned in the Bible.

Who was she? And how did she become so powerful? Born in a king's palace in Sidon across the Jordan, Jezebel learned that her seductive ways and strong will could manipulate men. A marriage of convenience was arranged by Ethbaal, her father, and she became the wife of Ahab, king of Israel.

Jezebel understood how to get what she wanted. Her power of persuasion involved a measure of physical beauty, manipulation, and, upon occasion, physical power. She destroyed anyone and everyone who stood in her way. Both men and women moved quickly to get away from her wrath.

In Israel, Jezebel introduced the worship of an agricultural deity, Baal, bringing in an Asherah pole and sexual expression as part of that worship. Eventually, human sacrifice was introduced, and archaeologists have unearthed the remains of tiny infant bones sealed in jars, hundreds of years old, a grim testimony to what took place.

There was, however, one man who withstood her fury. But even he was afraid of her. His name: Elijah. You can read about him in 1 Kings in the Old Testament. When confronted with this hideous situation, Elijah challenged Jezebel's false religious leaders and the historic battle of the true and the false took place on Mt. Carmel. But after the four hundred fifty prophets of Baal were eliminated, Jezebel vowed to kill Elijah like the prophets had been killed

Violence has a way of begetting violence! An eternal law of the harvest says that you reap what you sow. Eventually, Jezebel met her death in much the same manner as she accomplished her goals—violently and cruelly. Elijah, not given to flattery, prophesied that her end would be marked with violence. "Dogs will devour Jezebel by the wall of Jezreel" (1 Kings 21:23). When Jezebel was confronted with an invading army, according to Scripture, "she put on eye makeup, arranged her hair" and went out to dialogue with the enemy (2 Kings 9:30). This time, though, palace attendants turned the tables on her and threw her to her death, where dogs devoured her body, exactly as Elijah had predicted. The cosmetics she had used lay untouched in her palace for archaeologists to find thousands of years later.

EXHIBIT 5: Four Coins in the Pool of Siloam

Having never studied the Bible, the skeptic considers himself to be in a better position to determine what is factual and what is mythical than the dedicated scholar who has immersed himself in the study of Scripture for a lifetime. At least, that's what some believe.

Take, for example, the belief that the Pool of Siloam you read about in John 9 didn't really exist, and that the story was more like a parable or myth than a factual encounter. Says Princeton Theological Seminary professor Dr. James Charlesworth, "Scholars have said that there wasn't a Pool of Siloam and that John was using a religious 'conceit' to illustrate a point." But then something happened.

Workers digging up a sewer line in the Old City of Jerusalem uncovered two steps—something they didn't expect to find while repairing a sewer. Work stopped. The Israel Antiquities Authority was called in, and archaeologists started excavating. They knew they were on to something big, something important. As archaeologist Eli Shukron cleared the rubble he was 100 percent certain—this had to be the Pool of Siloam where the blind man was healed by Jesus.

How could they be so sure it was a first-century structure? Workers constructing the original pool had buried four coins in the plaster. All four bore images of Alexander Jannaeus, the Jewish king who ruled Jerusalem from 103 to 76 BC. Archaeologists also found another dozen coins dating from the period of the Jewish revolt against Rome from AD 66 to 70. That demonstrated for certain that the pool had been silted in or filled up by that time.

The Pool of Siloam, located near the gate of the old city where weary travelers could pause and refresh themselves, was the very pool to which the blind man was sent when Jesus healed him. Says Professor Charlesworth, "A gospel that was thought to be 'pure theology' is now shown to be grounded in history."[47] Forget about "Three Coins in a Fountain." I'll go with four coins in the Pool of Siloam—proof that was buried 2,000 years ago confirming the record of Scripture.

The Bottom Line

Archaeology consistently authenticates biblical statements regarding individuals, geographic locations, and historical events. The late Professor W. F. Albright, one of the twentieth century's most respected archaeologists and linguists, who taught Semitic languages at Johns Hopkins University from 1929 to 1958, wrote, "During the past century, our knowledge of the historical and literary background of the Bible has increased by a series of prodigious leaps, and it is now advancing with increasing speed."[48]

Science and technology have allowed archaeologists to better interpret the vast number of archaeological expeditions. "Phenomenal" is the word Professor Albright used to describe the scientific contribution of disciplines such as carbon isotope dating, DNA analysis, and satellite imaging.

Gradually, expedition by expedition, dig by dig, case by case we have increased our understanding of cultures, history, names, events, and places. And the greater our knowledge, the stronger is the bridge of confidence that the Bible contains accurate history. The individuals and events recorded in this text are represented exactly as they were—not fabricated composites, as some would have us believe. As Millar Burrows, a Yale University professor, puts it, "Archaeology has in many cases refuted the views of modern critics. It has shown in a number of instances that these views rest on false assumptions and unreal, artificial schemes of historical development."[49]

The evidence of archaeology, often intertwined with manuscript discoveries, forms a case for biblical truth that grows only stronger as time passes.

CHAPTER 4

THE TESTIMONY OF FULFILLED PROPHECY

There is only one real inevitability:
It is necessary that the Scripture be fulfilled.
Carl Henry[50]

In this chapter we are going to consider only two incidents that fulfilled prophecies made centuries ago–the birth of Jesus Christ, and what I consider to be the most significant fulfilled prophecy of the twentieth century: the birth of modern Israel.

Let's begin by confronting the possibility of both happening by chance. To what degree is chance involved when it comes to the laws of probability? If you answer, "Not much!" you are right, because the laws of probability are carefully defined and mathematically calculated. There is no real element of likelihood or chance whatsoever. For example, take a coin and toss it in the air. If the coin is perfectly balanced, it has a one in two chances of coming up heads, right? Now, what chance is there in it coming up heads twice in a row? The odds are one in four. Again, what chance is there of the coin coming up heads three times in a row? If you answer, "One chance in eight," you are right.

Now with this in mind, consider another question: Have you ever applied the laws of chance or probability to the remarkable prophecies which were made prior to the coming of Jesus Christ to earth? Dr. Charles Ryrie says, "Someone has calculated that actually there are more than 300 prophecies concerning various aspects of the first coming of Christ." Another scholar says that there are 332 prophecies relating to Jesus Christ, sixty-one of which are major prophecies.

To help you grasp the immense improbability of these being fulfilled by chance, let me give you something to think about. Let's begin by pondering the possibility of just eight of those being fulfilled. One college math class that investigated this likelihood concluded that it would be one possibility in ten to the seventeenth power. The chance of forty-eight of those being fulfilled is one in ten to the 157th power.[51]

When Jesus was here on earth, he had a keen sense of understanding that he was fulfilling the prophecies of old. The average person has little understanding of the complexity of prophecies and their importance when it comes to documenting what Jesus did. But Jesus stressed their importance. Immediately before the crucifixion

Jesus said, "I am telling you now before it happens, so that when it does happen you will believe that I am who I am" (John 13:19).

There were three prophecies, at least, over which Jesus Christ had absolutely no control this side of heaven:

- The place where he was born

- The time of his birth

- The manner in which he was born

The chance of these three being fulfilled, if it were as simple as tossing a coin in the air, would be one in sixteen, but the chances of these three prophecies being fulfilled in the detailed manner predicted goes far beyond chance. Simply put, in the natural world it could never have just happened.

The Place of His Birth

At least 500 years before Jesus was born, Micah predicted the village where his birth would take place. He wrote, "But you, Bethlehem Ephrathah, though you are small among the clans of Judah, out of you will come for me one who will be ruler over Israel, whose origins are from of old, from ancient times" (Micah 5:2). Jesus being born in Bethlehem to a descendant of David (whose home was in this same Judean village of Bethlehem) fulfilled the prophecy made centuries before.

The Timing of His Birth

The events leading to the birth of Jesus were much like the components of a fine Swiss watch consisting of a variety of cogs, springs, and gears working with synchronicity so that the hands of the watch are trustworthy. Some of those events surrounding his birth were relatively minor, and some were major, but timing was everything. Thus Paul, looking back over the series of occurrences which had to come together, wrote, "But when the set time had fully come, God sent his Son, born of a woman, born under the law" (Galatians 4:4).

The scenario had begun many years before the birth of the infant Jesus, when Julius Caesar was assassinated in 44 BC and his grandnephew Augustus became Caesar. Considered weak by most Roman senators, Augustus teamed up with Mark Antony and Marcus Lepidus and purged the senate, ensuring he had a powerful grip on his future.

Augustus was no different from politicians today. He wanted to leave behind a legacy in marble and stone, and to get the money for his beautification program, he did what politicians still do—tax the people! Luke tells us,

> "In those days Caesar Augustus issued a decree that a census should be taken of the entire Roman world. (This was the first census that took place while Quirinius was governor of Syria.) And everyone went

to their own town to register. So Joseph also went up from the town of Nazareth in Galilee to Judea, to Bethlehem the town of David, because he belonged to the house and line of David." (Luke 2:1–4)

Once the decree was given, a messenger made his way from Rome to the harbor at Puteoli. From there he boarded a ship, taking the order across the Mediterranean—a journey of six to eight weeks depending on the vagaries of winds and currents. Had the decree not been given ordering men to register in their ancestral homes (Bethlehem, for Joseph, because he was a descendant of David), a poor carpenter would never have undertaken a journey of this distance with a wife well more than eight months pregnant.

Furthermore, some six centuries before Christ was born, Daniel prophesied an elaborate time table (Daniel 9:24–27) that seems to pinpoint the exact time sequence leading to his birth—something so phenomenal that only God could have known this.

In order for the details of Jesus' birth to fulfill the prophecies made centuries before, the timing had to be precise. The pace that the ship was borne on the waves, the speed at which the order was posted in Palestine, and even the pace of the journey that brought Mary and Joseph to Bethlehem—all of this, of course, had to synchronize with the timing of Mary's pregnancy for prophecy to come to pass. Had any of these events leading to the birth of Christ taken only a few days longer—say, for instance, had the winds which bore the ship blown a bit more sharply—Jesus would have been born in Nazareth, where Joseph lived, rather than in Bethlehem. You begin to see immediately that the chance of just three of these prophecies happening is remarkable.

The Manner of His Birth

"Therefore the Lord himself will give you a sign: The virgin will conceive and give birth to a son, and will call him Immanuel," wrote Isaiah the prophet (Isaiah 7:14). "Does it really matter whether or not Jesus was born of a virgin?" If Jesus Christ was not born of a virgin, Christians of all faiths have been misled for 2,000 years, and obviously, Matthew and Luke were deceived as well. Neither Matthew nor Luke were writing poetical couplets, but literally telling what transpired—an event celebrated by all Christendom every December 25.

Luke was a doctor, a Syrian physician, who had been at the side of scores of women who brought infants into the world. I acknowledge that a doctor can be a poet, but when Dr. Luke wrote to Theophilus and described the birth of Jesus, he was being as factual as he would have been in filling out a birth certificate. He says plainly that the angel appeared to Mary, who was a virgin, and when the angel told her that she would bear a son, she objected, asking quite directly, "How will this be . . . since I am a virgin?" (Luke 1:34).

Matthew was a tax collector turned disciple of Jesus Christ, who wasn't accustomed to poetic license when he filled in the tax ledger he kept for the provincial government. In the book which bears his name, Matthew makes careful note of details, something I would expect a tax collector to do, as he accurately traces the lineage of Joseph back to Abraham, the father of the Jewish race. He records father-and-son relationships until he gets to Jesus' father and then he switches genders: "Jacob was the father of Joseph the husband of Mary, by whom Jesus was born, who is called the Messiah" (Matthew 1:16 NASB).

Interestingly, Matthew doesn't say Jesus was born of Joseph, the pattern he followed with all the previous generations. He used a feminine gender in the Greek text, and says, "Of Mary was born Christ," leaving Joseph's DNA entirely out of the picture as to being the actual father of Jesus.

Even critics have to admit that Matthew and Luke believed Jesus was born of a virgin. The early church fathers were convinced that the event of Jesus' birth in Bethlehem was the intersection of man and God in a unique being who was both fully man and fully God. They debated it, sought to understand it, but never denied it. It was part of the very fabric of Christianity which was recognized not only by the Church but also by Muslims.

Does it really matter today whether or not Jesus was born of a virgin? If fulfilled prophecy is important, the reality of the virgin birth is an issue of primary concern. If Christianity matters, the virgin birth of Christ matters greatly. Great men have died as martyrs, but our redemption could take place only in the death of a sinless man whose lineage was not tainted with human failure and sin.

When God detailed the circumstances relating to the coming of his son, he was making the odds so great that it was absolutely impossible for them to have "just happened." Knowing this truth could strengthen your confidence in what the Word says.

The Bottom Line

The prophecies of the Bible clearly foretelling events, naming individuals, and even predicting dates are accurately verified by history and thereby attest to the supernatural character of this book. When you make a prediction, you are either right or wrong! And getting it entirely right is the acid test of whether or not God has spoken through a prophet. Moses said that if a man is really a prophet with insights which have come through the revelation of the Holy Spirit, there is no room for error. He's either 100 percent right, or else he is not a prophet. Thus he wrote, "If what a prophet proclaims in the name of the LORD does not take place or come true, that is a message the LORD has not spoken" (Deuteronomy 18:22), and God instructed that the person should forfeit his life. Pretty strong action. These so-called prophets could be dead wrong, literally!

No other book in the world has so many explicit and detailed prophecies as to events in the future that can be readily pronounced "fulfilled!"—verified by history—as does the Bible.

Wrote the late D. James Kennedy,

In all the writings of Buddha, Confucius, and Lao-tse, you will not find a single example of predicted prophecy. In the Koran (the writings of Muhammad) there is one instance of a specific prophecy—a self-fulfilling prophecy that he, Muhammad himself, would return to Mecca. Quite different from the prophecy of Jesus who said that He would return from the grave. One is easily fulfilled, and the other is impossible to any human being.[52]

The Development of Modern Israel

This event was the most significant fulfilled prophecy of the twentieth century. It was September, 1967—barely ninety days after the Six-Day War—when I visited Israel for the first time. Taking a small tape recorder, I interviewed as many people as I could, asking a basic question: "How do you account for the remarkable victory that Israel won?" Taxi drivers, tourist guides, government workers, soldiers in uniform, and people on the street all were quick to relate how the odds were stacked against them. Fifty million Arabs were intent on driving some two millions Jews into the Mediterranean. But there was singular and unanimous agreement. "God gave us the victory," they said. Forget about military hardware, superior equipment, better strategy, or bravado.

Hardened soldiers told me their parents had been victims of the Holocaust and that they had not wept openly from the day their parents were taken from them until the day they stood at the Western Wall of the temple; but as they stood on the perimeter of what had once been the foundation of the temple, something inexplicable happened, something deep inside broke up in a flood of tears and emotions.

What is the fascination with this piece of stone wall about 150 feet long and 90 feet high—the remnant of the foundation of the first-century temple—overlooking the Kidron Valley? Here stood the temple originally built by Solomon, destroyed by the Babylonians, rebuilt following the captivity under Zerubbabel, then enlarged and refurbished by Herod the Great around 20 BC. On this spot, the Holy of Holies and the ark of the covenant stood. It was sacred ground, the meeting place of God and man.

You might also wonder, "What's so special about Israel?" It's not a large country—just a narrow piece of land sandwiched between the Mediterranean Sea and the Arabian Desert. Yet, the establishment of the modern state of Israel and how it came about, when never before in all history has a people so scattered across the surface of the earth come back to their roots, constitutes one of the most astonishing and remarkable prophecies of Scripture, one fulfilled in the past century.

To understand why the re-establishment of Israel is significant, you need to know something of the historical developments. Following the destruction of Jerusalem in AD 70 when the temple was demolished, the Jewish people were spread across the face of the earth—some going into Egypt, some to Europe, some to Asia; and wherever they went they took the Torah, or Old Testament Scriptures, and for centuries observed the Passover with the words, "Next year in Jerusalem!" That hope never died.

Meanwhile Jerusalem was overthrown some forty-three times by various and assorted armies, including waves of Crusaders in the Middle Ages intent on driving infidels from the holy places.

In 1897, however, God significantly used an unlikely person, an atheist named Theodore Herzyl, to convene the first Jewish Congress in Basil, Switzerland. From all over the world, prominent Jews came to talk about how wonderful it would be to have a homeland for the Jewish people.

Victor Hugo once said, "Nothing in all the world is as powerful as an idea whose time has come," and his words described the quickening impulse in the hearts of Jews to immigrate to this tiny territory between Lebanon and Syria on the north and Egypt on the west. Then a trickle of immigrants returned to the land their ancestors had once fled, buying what Arab locals consider to be worthless pieces of property—often swampy land infested with mosquitoes and malaria—for inflated prices. Those who sold land to the emigrant Jews later sat in coffee houses laughing at the ridiculous prices they had been paid for the desolate land. Their smiles, however, soon faded as they watched the Jews, undaunted, drain the swamps, plant trees, dig out rocks, and plow the ground—often physically pulling the plow behind them. Frequently fighting disease and sickness, the immigrant Jews gradually gained a toe-hold on this land that was once taken by Joshua.

At the same time, a lad by the name of Arthur James Balfour was growing up in Britain. He attended the local Anglican church, where an evangelical rector told his parishioners that the Bible says eventually the Jews will return to their promised land. That thought was planted in Balfour's mind, and he never forgot it.

Then World War I broke out, taking the lives of thirteen million people, and in the aftermath of this conflict, anti-Semitism reared its ugly head as failed politicians blamed the Jews—especially the bankers and industrialists—for the post-war economic failure. As the war was winding down, General Allenby, leading the British troops, routed the Turks from Jerusalem and rode into the city on a white horse. He saw himself as a liberator.

In the mandate bringing resolution to the war, Lord Balfour, then the British Prime Minister, persuaded the British crown that it was in the interest of Her Majesty's government to establish a homeland for the Jewish people. Thus Lord Balfour was responsible for the adoption of a position paper known as a White Paper. It carried no legal clout but was an expression of the good will of the British government. It read that it was "pleasing to Her Majesty's government to allow the Jewish people to have a homeland." That was 1917. And the creation of the paper known as The Balfour Declaration became a significant and meaningful step towards the creation of the modern state of Israel.

The aftermath of the war created almost unbearably harsh conditions in Germany. The economy was in shambles, and reparations caused unrest among the people. Adolf Hitler, then a student in Vienna—according to a story disputed by some and embraced by many—was walking down the street one day, when a Jewish rabbi, wearing the traditional black garb, side curls dangling over a book he was reading, didn't see the young student and bumped into him. Losing his balance, Adolph fell into a mud puddle. Rising to his feet, Hitler shook his fist at the rabbi, cursing him and vowing that some day he would kill every Jew in Europe.

Exactly how the bitter cauldron of anti-Semitism was born in the heart of this young man may never be fully known, but his legacy of hatred—a demonic kind that knows no logic or sense—resulted in embroiling the whole world in a devastating conflict.

Some six million Jews died in the concentration camps of Europe, for Hitler was intent on wiping out a race who had been made the scapegoats of Germany's failed economy.

Today, memorials to those who died are found in such places as Auschwitz and nearby Birkenau, Dachau, and Mauthausen. Yet until you see a map showing the vast network of concentration camps numbering in the hundreds, you would have no idea of the horrible extent of the Holocaust.

Following the end of World War II, Zionists were offered land for the establishment of a Jewish homeland in Argentina and elsewhere. But other locations were not the same! The hearts of Jews all over the world, both religious and secular, were drawn to the place where Abraham offered his son on Mt. Moriah, and the city of David, where the great temple built by Solomon had stood. This was their land, so they reasoned, and they wanted it back.

Meanwhile, Eliezer Ben-Yehuda, a Lithuanian Jew, moved to Jerusalem. Upon arriving in the Holy Land, he determined to speak nothing but Hebrew—the same

Hebrew spoken by Isaiah and the prophets. Yiddish, a mishmash of Hebrew German and Balto-Slavic spoken by most Jews in Eastern Europe, was not the language of the book, he declared. "When his first son, Ben-Zion Ben Ychuda (or, as he is more commonly known, Ittamar Ben-Avi), was born in 1882, Ben-Yehuda made his wife, Deborah, promise to raise the boy as the first all-Hebrew speaking child in modern history," writes Jack Fellman.[53] He single-handedly waged a battle to give biblical Hebrew a rebirth—a first in the history of the world that a language fell into disuse and was resurrected.

When there were no Hebrew words to describe such things as "plastic" or other items with no adequate equivalent, Ben-Yahuda coined them. They became standard usage for modern Hebrew. And he succeeded, with Hebrew eventually becoming the official language of Israel. Should Elijah or Daniel be resurrected and walk down Dizengoff Street in Tel Aviv on a Saturday night, following the end of Sabbath, he could read the menu at a local restaurant and eat his meal while he read the weekend edition of the Jerusalem Post—in the same language spoken centuries before.

Finally, the tide of public opinion turned, and at four p.m. on May 14, 1948, just before the Sabbath began, David Ben-Gurion walked to the podium in the Museum of Art on Rothschild Boulevard in Tel Aviv and, with a voice that was steady and firm but fueled by intense emotion, read a Declaration of Independence, announcing the establishment of a Jewish nation to be known as the State of Israel. Inside that room were 200 people who saw history made. They applauded, then wept, then spontaneously broke into singing *Hatikvah* ("hope"), which was to become the national anthem. Outside a vast crowd of people had massed. Soldiers on the roof, Sten machine guns ready, scanned the crowd for terrorists. Even as Ben-Gurion spoke, gunfire erupted outside, and the War of Liberation was on.

How Does the Modern State of Israel Relate to Fulfilled Prophecy?

Some seven centuries before Christ, Isaiah recorded an amazing prophecy, and one powerful phrase of the prophecy certifies this indescribable tug in the hearts of Jews all over the world to come back to this desolate, arid country. Isaiah said,

> In that day the Lord will reach out his hand *a second time* to reclaim the surviving remnant of his people from Assyria, from Lower Egypt, from Upper Egypt, from Cush, from Elam, from Babylonia, from Hamath and from the islands of the Mediterranean. (Isaiah 11:11, italics added)

Let's go back and take a closer look at how this prophecy was fulfilled. In 603 BC, Nebuchadnezzar, king of

Babylon, laid siege to Jerusalem and eventually destroyed the city (586 BC), taking the finest of the youth back to Babylon. The prophet Jeremiah, who had predicted the destruction of the city, gave specifics when he said they would be in captivity for seventy years. He wrote,

> "This whole country will become a desolate wasteland, and these nations will serve the king of Babylon seventy years. But when the seventy years are fulfilled, I will punish the king of Babylon and his nation, the land of the Babylonians, for their guilt," declares the LORD, "and will make it desolate forever." (Jeremiah 25:11–12)

The day eventually came when the great Tigris River flowing through the city of Babylon was diverted, and while the king partied, the armies of the Medes and Persians crept under the city walls through the dry bed of the Tigris, overthrew the garrison and took the city. Wanting to placate some of the subjects, Cyrus, the new king, issued a decree allowing the Jews to return seventy years after the captivity.

When they returned to their homeland under Ezra and Nehemiah, that was Isaiah's *first* return. There was no second recorded in history until the twentieth century, when a gradual exodus resulted in plane after plane of exiles from all over the world coming back to till the land once trod by the patriarchs.

In my library is a nondescript little book of seventy-four pages that my father-in-law, Guy P. Duffield, had acquired secondhand, and I eventually inherited from him. The price on the inside cover tells me it sold for sixty cents when it was written in 1941. Its intrinsic value is limited; however, I smile every time I take down the book and browse through it. Why? 1941 is the year remembered by us who are Americans for the Japanese attack on Pearl Harbor on December 7. The next day, December 8, the US Congress declared war on Japan. A mere three days later Germany declared war on the US, which meant the US became involved in Europe. Prior to those fateful days, though, Dr. Harry Rimmer, a Presbyterian pastor, archaeologist, scientist, and staunch defender of the faith, wrote this book I now own entitled *Palestine: The Coming Storm Center.*

Rimmer believed that coming events cast their shadow before them, and based upon Ezekiel 37–39 and other Old Testament prophecies, he saw Israel as a nation that would be reborn with great travail. The premise of his book is that Palestine was about to become embroiled in major conflict involving much of the world and that the conflict would culminate in the establishment of the modern state of Israel.

What makes Rimmer's book a source of mirth, though, are the notations written in the margins of the pages by a skeptic who disbelieved what Rimmer had written. Comments include the following: "Who says?" "Silly reasoning." "Dogmatic." "Monstrous reasoning," and so forth.

Rimmer concludes his book by saying,

> So the storm which Ezekiel foretold is even now gathering, and no man can say when it will break! The only certainty is that it will come, and it may be very soon. But this will not be the last world attempt to blot out the Jew.
>
> As the dark clouds of the final storm gather before our very eyes, may God grant that we shall not be taken unaware by the swift flight of events. When the hearts of natural men are literally fainting with the fear of what the future may unfold, we can lift up our heads, knowing that Jesus is coming again, and our redemption is nearly complete.
>
> Even so, Lord Jesus, come quickly![54]

When the skeptic penned words in the margins reflecting his incredulity, he was blind to the dark, ominous clouds that were settling over Europe at that very time which would bring the cauldron of hatred against the Jews to a boiling point resulting in the horrors of the Holocaust.

What Harry Rimmer wrote in 1941 was fulfilled on May 14, 1947 when an Israeli flag was raised on Mt. Zion, fulfilling biblical prophecy to the letter!

Can You Trust the Bible?

CHAPTER 5

THE TRUCE WITH SCIENCE

*Looking at the doctrine of Darwinism which
undergirded my atheism for so many years, it didn't
take me long to conclude that it was simply too
far-fetched to be credible.*

Lee Strobel[55]

When Moses wrote the first sentence in the book of Genesis, he began by penning the words, "In the beginning God created the heavens and the earth." In writing those words, Moses broke with accepted Hebrew grammar in how he recorded the first phrase, "in the beginning." Proper grammar is to link the phrase to something like "in the beginning of (whatever)" but Moses knew there was no antecedent or precedent to attach that phrase to, so literally he says, "In beginning, God!" That's it! He assumes God's existence. There is no footnote striving to establish proofs of his existence. He's there. He has always been there and always will be, contended Moses.

Blaise Pascal, the French scientist and theologian, put it,

> "Either God exists, or he does not." But which side shall we take? Reason cannot decide for us one way or the other; we are separated by an infinite gulf.... Let us weigh the gain and the loss in betting that God exists.... If you win, you win everything; if you lose, you lose nothing. Do not hesitate then, to gamble on His existence.

Seemingly, the deeper the probe of science, the closer we come to the reality of the God who spoke the Word and brought our world into being. The Cosmic Background Explorer satellite, which was put into orbit as part of the US space program, confirms that immediately following what scientists refer to as the "Big Bang," there were ripples of matter that seemed to form in patterns. But what was observed was not a chaotic explosion such as follows when you put a firecracker under a tin can or in an ant hill, but a systematic pattern that reflects design.

Moses not only began with the premise that there is God, but that this One was the Creator of what we live on and what we see. It is the argument posed by the story of one who is walking a trail in the mountains who crosses a stream and encounters three large rocks stacked one upon another. All three are approximately the same size and of the same composition. So what does it mean? Who put them there? Is this a trail marker made by someone in the long distant past? Is it a warning that the traveler should not proceed further? Whatever the answer to these questions, it is obvious that these three rocks did not happen to align themselves by chance. Someone was responsible for their being placed where they were, and all the earthquakes the Rim of Fire can produce would not so position them this way.

The gifted intellectual Samuel Johnson spent nine years of his life producing his *Dictionary of the English Language*. One of his biographers described him as "a genius—a man with a computer-like memory and a mind that could assemble, analyze, organize and present ideas so uniquely that the greatest people of his day clamored to sit and listen to him." Do you think that anyone could ever be convinced that the dictionary which bears Johnson's name was the result of an explosion in a London print shop when someone forgot to turn off the gas lamp? No, of course not!

Here's one last absurdity to ponder: The Eiffel Tower in Paris rises some 984 feet into the air. When it was built for the exposition of 1889, it was considered to be one of the greatest engineering feats of all time. It contains some 7,000 tons of iron and steel, and for many years was the highest structure in the world. You could never convince Alexandre Gustave Eiffel that it just happened to exist because the idea for the magnificent tower first existed in his mind. Eventually, he developed his idea on paper. Then the idea evolved into blueprints which eventually became a reality.

Evidence for creation lies all around us: the complexity of the human body, including our emotional make-up; the fine-tuned precision of the solar system; the laws of thermodynamics; the ongoing exploration of the solar system; the laws of chemistry, which allow two atoms of hydrogen and one of oxygen, both combustible, to combine and form a molecule of water which extinguishes fire.

The Response of Darwinian Atheism

How do you discount the argument that design demands a designer? A group of scientists and philosophers argues that everything can be explained by natural causes—including the concept of God. Leading the group who charge that a belief in the supernatural and anything going beyond nature is passé is the Oxford professor Richard Dawkins, author of the book *The God Delusion.* In his book, Dawkins attacks belief in a creator, contending that anyone who believes in the miraculous has lost any scientific credibility.

In a debate with Francis Collins, the genome pioneer who headed a multinational team of 2,400 scientists that mapped the three billion biochemical letters of our genetic blueprint, Dawkins attempted to explain how he thought Darwinism could have produced a seemingly "designed" product:

> For centuries the most powerful argument for God's existence from the physical world was the so-called argument from design: Living things are so beautiful and elegant and so apparently purposeful, they could only have been made by an intelligent designer. But Darwin provided a simpler explanation. His way is a gradual incremental improvement starting from very simple beginnings and working up step by tiny incremental step to more complexity, more elegance, more adaptive perfection. Each step is not too improbable to countenance, but when you add them up cumulatively over millions of years, you get these monsters of improbability, like the human brain and the rain forest. It should warn us against ever assuming that because something is complicated, God must have designed it.[56]

Collins rebutted the logic of his opponent, saying, "I actually find the argument of the existence of a God who did the planning more compelling ... less a stretching of the imagination."[57]

Physicist Charles H. Townes, who won the 1964 Nobel Prize for his work on lasers, explains that a person must have faith whether he or she believes in creation as an act of God or as a random act of chance. In *Think* magazine, then published by IBM, he says,

> Faith is essential to science too, although we do not generally recognize the basic need and nature of faith in science. Faith is necessary for the scientist even to get started, and deep faith necessary for him to carry out his tougher tasks. Why? Because he must have confidence that there is order in the universe and that the human mind—in fact, his own mind—has a good chance of understanding this order.[58]

The Argument from a Mousetrap

"If it could be demonstrated that any complex organ existed, which could not possibly have been formed by numerous, successive, slight modifications, my theory would absolutely break down," wrote Charles Darwin in *Origin of Species*.[59] If Darwin were alive today, it is well possible that Darwin would rethink his premise of natural selection.

What's happened? A simple mousetrap—yes, the kind that I have in my garage to control the vermin which slip under the door intent on making their home there—was part of the logic which eventually caused an unassuming looking microbiologist named Michael Behe to rethink the logical steps or building blocks of life. And what does a mousetrap have to do with the building blocks of DNA and life? Simply put, a mousetrap consists of five parts that must each function independently and be in place for the simple apparatus to work. Likewise, theorized Behe, for life to be sustained, certain systems had to function and operate all at the same time. Behe was not out on an anti-evolution, pro-creation crusade at all. He is a simple man who finally held Darwin accountable and discovered he had come up short. Behe calls it "irreducible complexity."

After pointing out the fact that a mousetrap consists of five simple but necessary parts, he says,

> You need all the parts to catch a mouse. You can't catch a few mice with a platform, then add the spring and catch a few more, and then add the hammer and improve its function. All the parts must be there to have any function at all. The mousetrap is irreducibly complex.

And as a microbiologist who takes apart the building blocks of DNA, he is convinced that certain systems had to be working and in place for life to have been sustained.

In his ground-breaking book *Darwin's Black Box*, he says,

> To Darwin, the cell was a "black box"—its inner workings were utterly mysterious to him. Now the black box has been opened up and we know how it works. Applying Darwin's test to the ultra-complex

world of molecular machinery and cellular systems that have been discovered over the past forty years, we can say that Darwin's theory has "absolutely broken down."

Behe further says, "The question for evolution is not whether you can take a mousetrap and use its parts for something else; it's whether you can start with something else and make it into a mousetrap."[60]

And, of course, the entire scientific community readily recognizes the truth of what Behe is saying, right? Well, not exactly. Some Darwinists have praised the author for his insightful analysis—not quite sure what to say or to make of it but recognizing that the molecular biologist's findings cannot simply be dismissed. Others simply denounce him as being unscientific.

Michael Behe, who dislikes being labeled a creationist, believes that God—not chance—was the Intelligent Designer. And he stresses that "science itself may not have the ability to ferret out the identity of the designer any more than astronomers can determine from their measurements the one who caused the expanding universe to spring into being out of nothing." Behe believes that neither science nor religion should usurp the other. Nor does he see them as being in conflict with each other.

Some, such as Louis Pasteur, have completely compartmentalized science and religion, seeing no interaction between the two. Others, however, do recognize the interaction. Charles H. Townes, the Nobel Prize-winning physicist previously quoted, has written,

> Some accept both religion and science as dealing with quite different matters by different methods, and thus separate them so widely in their thinking that no direct confrontation is possible. Some repair rather completely to the camp of science or of religion and regard the other as ultimately of little importance, if not downright harmful. To me science and religion are both universal, and basically very similar.[61]

Francis Collins agrees with that premise. In an interview with John Horgan, Collins said, "The God of the Bible is also the God of the genome. He can be worshiped in the cathedral or in the laboratory."[62]

Resolving the Conflict between the Bible and Scicnce

Yale psychologist Paul Bloom says, "Religion and science will always clash." He has a lot of history on his side, but the issue is this: Can the tension between science and religion be resolved? If so, how is resolution possible? That was the issue that confronted a former British chaplain who did a doctorate at Oxford following World War II. In his lifetime, J. Edwin Orr received eleven graduate degrees, including degrees from the University of South Africa, Semaphore University in India, and two doctorates from the University of California in Los Angeles (UCLA).

Orr held to the premise that there is one God—not two, a God of the Bible and a god of science—and that this sovereign God has revealed his words in Scripture and his works in science. He rejected the premise that science and faith occupy two separate, airtight boxes with no interactions between them.

Orr reasoned that God's word has been recorded in the Bible in passages (texts). But going beyond the statement recorded in Scripture is what men say the Bible says, which is an interpretation of the text. Orr wouldn't argue for the validity of interpretations of Scripture (for example, the duration of creation) but rather the textual statement that "In the beginning God created the heavens and the earth."

On the other side of the paradigm, Orr contends that God's awesome works are the subject of science—what nature reveals—the "what happened" of our world, and when something can clearly be demonstrated and proved, it ceases to be theory and must be recognized as a scientific fact. But the extension of the fact into the realm of possibility or probability is a scientific theory.

"The sky is blue because that's the way God made it," says the Christian. "The sky is blue because of wavelength dependence of Rayleigh scattering," says the scientist on the other side of the issue. So, are these two statements in conflict and, therefore, contradictory? Not really. The first statement describes the color observed by the naked eye. But the other statement describes *why* the sky is blue. Both are correct. The Bible deals with the *what*; science deals with the *how*.

The logic of Orr's paradigm can be visualized as follows:

ONE GOD
who has revealed his

WORD	WORKS
in the	in
BIBLE	**SCIENCE**

TEXTS → FACTS
INTERPRET → THEORIES

What people *say* the Bible says (which is often pushed beyond the actual statement of the biblical text) and what it *really* says often contradict each other. Likewise, the same conflict is present when theories are presumed to be factual. Any premise that can be logically verified under the same set of circumstances anywhere ceases to be a theory and can legitimately be recognized as factual. But when theories are considered factual (i.e., "Doesn't everyone believe that evolution is factual?") and those theories contradict the actual statements of Scripture, there is unresolved tension.

What's the solution? Orr believed the conflict is resolved by ensuring that the theories of science are cross-checked with the factual statements of biblical text, and the interpretations of Scripture are cross-checked with demonstrable facts of science.

The Genesis account of creation states that God created the heavens and the earth, and the Hebrew word *bara*, translated "to create," is used at three critical junctures in the text—the creation of matter, the creation of lower forms of life, and the creation of human life (Genesis 1:1, 21, and 27, respectively). The word generally means "to create from no previous existing materials," and it is here that the biblical account and Darwinian evolution stand in sharp opposition to each other.[63]

Moses' contention that God was the cause of creation has the finality of a stake driven into the ground without reference to how long it took,[64] the manner in which he did it, or the full extent of what happened.

"So God created mankind . . . " wrote Moses. George Gallup, the man who gained fame as a poll taker, has said, "I could prove God statistically. Take the human body alone. The chance that all the functions of the individual would just happen is a statistical monstrosity."

For a few moments, consider the intricacies of your body.

- Let us start with your brain—the control center of your body. It weighs about three pounds (two percent of the weight of your body) and consists of 100 billion neurons in two major hemispheres connected by a broad, thick band of fibers—a kind of interface known as the corpus collosum. Thousands of thoughts pass in and out of your mind every day. Your brain has storage vaults that contain bits of information recorded years before. Yet as an average person you use less than 10 percent of your brain. No computer has ever been invented that comes even close to rivaling the powers of the brain. (After all, who invented computers?) In spite of the marriage of science and technology in the past centuries, the human brain has been called the last frontier of science, and only in the 1990s did scientists begin to unravel its marvels and its interaction with the rest of our bodies.

- Then, there is that organ in your body about the size of a man's fist called the heart. It is a muscle that contracts and forces blood through over 60,000 miles of veins, arteries and capillaries, pulsating 100,000 times every day. It pumps about seventy-five gallons of blood every hour or 1,800 gallons every day. Simple math shows that working 24/7, it pumps 12,600 gallons a week or 50,000 gallons every month.[65]

- No camera ever invented comes even close to the intricacies of the human eye, with an iris that automatically adjusts to different lighting and has a lubrication system that allows dust or grime to be whisked away with a blink. Your eyes are also protected by eyelashes—some 200 hairs per eye that last from three to five months before you grow a new set of them.

- Bose speakers are considered to be some of the world's finest (at least among the world's higher priced ones), yet no laboratory in the world can produce the stereo system you were born with, one that detects sound waves at a frequency of about sixteen to 20,000 cycles per second. Your ears are hard-wired to your brain, which gives you a special reference to what you hear because sound arrives in one ear a hundredth of a second before it reaches the other ear.

- No air conditioning system has ever been designed to be as efficient as the one that keeps the body's thermostat at a steady 98.6 degrees Fahrenheit when it's working right and sends chills or fever when the system is threatened by disease.

- Your nervous system links all the systems of your body, advising the brain of what is happening, monitoring feelings, sensations, pain, and pleasure. Each of the 100 billion neurons in your nervous system is comprised of three parts. Dendrites receive information from another cell and transmit the message to the cell body. The cell body stores the information for retrieval, and the axon conducts messages away from the cell body.[66] Nerves in different parts of your body—the tongue, for example—are specialized to perform certain tasks.

- Your skeletal system forms a framework that anatomically adapts to your movement, whether you are a graceful ballerina on a stage or a pole-vaulter arching your body over the high bar. No bridge ever built surpasses the symmetry of the arch in your foot.

- Dr. Paul Brand, the renowned missionary surgeon famous for his research and reconstructive inventiveness helping lepers become functional, used to say that the hand is the epitome of God's creative genius—unduplicated by science. Rotate your hand, flexing your fingers, and compare what you see with the mechanical hands attached to a robot.

In the image of God he created them;
male and female he created them.[67]

But what does it mean when the text says that humankind is created in the image of God (Genesis 1:27)? Does that include the baby you brought into the world, as well as your gray-haired, feeble grandfather who talks about "going home and being with the Lord"?

Dr. Paul Brand, along with co-author Philip Yancey, argues that not only is the physical body an amazing creation that could never have happened by chance, but that the spirit of man is what really testifies loudly to the contention that we are created in the image of God. In his book *In His Image*, Dr. Brand wrote,

Yet increasingly I have come to realize that the physical shell I devote so much energy to is not the whole person. My patients are not mere collections of tendons, muscles, hair follicles, nerve cells, and skin cells. Each of them, regardless of deformed appearance and physical damage, contains an immortal spirit and is a vessel of the image of God.[68]

In every war, and every crisis, including the heroic response of police, firemen, and rescue workers following the 9/11 World Trade Center disaster, there are individuals who demonstrate they were created in the image of God by their actions. The chaplain who goes back into a building to pray with someone crushed under the wreckage, the passerby who stops at an accident and crawls into a burning vehicle to pull someone to safety, or the observer who plunges into a raging river to rescue a child being swept away with the current—they are the heroes in an often selfish, "me-first" world. "Created in the image of God" explains human kindness in ways that are not reflected by lower forms of life or explained by science.

In a world which threatens to reduce your uniqueness and individuality to a digital imprint or the black strip of information on the reverse side of a credit card, it is time to acknowledge you are a unique individual created in the image of God—fully human and with a soul that will live forever.

Walk through a museum and view the magnificent paintings of the masters and see the image of God reflected in their works. How else explain what came from the brushes of Rembrandt, Michelangelo, or Van Gogh? Read some of the great literature that fills the shelves—the classics. Read a sonnet from Shakespeare, a poem from Longfellow.

Listen to the music of George Frideric Handel, a symphony from Beethoven, or a stanza called "Amazing Grace," written by a slave trader turned minister, and you will see these expressions of beauty mirror the image of the Almighty. At the same time, remember that response to music, the delicate fragrance of a rose, the love of another person, the beauty of our world, and the pathos of someone who suffers all argue compellingly that you were created in the image of God—a composite of body, soul, and spirit.

While you may not be the "spittin' image" of your Father, you will see within your life the reflection of the image of God, the Father. That's what sets you apart from the rest of God's created beings—that demonstrates you are a living soul and spirit, not an animal. It is the spiritual nature of humankind that separates him from all other mammals and defies simple explanations that humans are the result of natural selection—mere chance that evolved from lower forms of life.

What about Scientific Statements in the Bible?

While the Bible is not a book on science but rather a book on life and living, what biblical writers penned centuries ago is in harmony with what we now consider to be scientific. At the time, what they wrote must have seemed strange to those who heard or read their comments. Their statements were often in sharp contrast to the scientific thought of the writer's day.

Consider the following:

Who Told Moses God Did It?

Take, for example, what Moses said about creation. The New Testament quotes Stephen, saying that Moses was schooled in "the wisdom of the Egyptians" (Acts 7:22). From secular history we know that the Egyptians of the fourteenth to twelfth century BC, the era in which Moses lived, believed that the earth was hatched from an egg. If you question that fertility model, check out the number of eggs on ancient sarcophagi and tombs in Egypt. Moses, though, didn't advance the egg theory. He said, "In the beginning God created the heavens and the earth."

"The World Is Round"—Really?

"Come on, now," you may say. "Doesn't everyone believe today that the world is round?" Surprisingly, no. The oldest continuous society in the world, having begun in 1547, is—are you ready for this?—the Flat Earth Society. Their website says they are "deprogramming the masses . . . dedicated to the Flat Earth principles which define our organization." A 1980 *Science Digest* magazine quoted the president of the society, Charles K. Johnson, as saying, "The facts are simple. The earth is flat!"[69]

The person who now serves as spokesman for this group lives in the shadow of Rockwell International, where the Space Shuttle was built, and a short distance across the rolling hills of Southern California from Edwards Air Force Base, where numerous Space Shuttles have landed. "The Space Shuttle is a joke—and a very ludicrous joke," he says. No, he's not kidding. He believes it. Seven centuries before Christ, the prophet Isaiah wrote these words: "He [God] sits enthroned above the circle of the earth, and its people are like grasshoppers" (Isaiah 40:22). Isaiah lived during a period when the Persian astronomers were convinced that the Earth was flat. But not Isaiah. In a written statement, Columbus said he got the idea of a round Earth from reading Isaiah's writings.[70]

"But," you say, "doesn't the Bible talk about the 'four corners' of the Earth?" Yes, the book of Revelation uses that term twice, denoting the broad expanse of the world's population—a figure of speech familiar to the readers. And that's the "flat-out truth."

How Many Stars Are Out There?

One of the interesting facts about the statements of a scientific nature which the writers of Scripture made about our world is that they were usually in sharp contrast to the philosophic or scientific ideas of their day. Nowhere is this more apparent than when Jeremiah made the statement found in the book that bears his name: "I will make the descendants of David my servant and the Levites who minister before me as countless as the stars of the sky and as measureless as the sand on the seashore" (Jeremiah 33:22).

That statement—that the stars cannot be numbered—was contrary to the wisdom of the ancient astronomers, but ultimately science demonstrated how right Jeremiah really was. As late as 150 BC (even several hundred years after Jeremiah), the Greek astronomer Hipparchus said there were 1026 stars in the universe. A hundred and fifty year later, Ptolemy, a Roman scientist who was alive at the time of Christ, said, "No! Hold it. There are not 1026 stars . . . but 1056 stars."

That wisdom held sway until AD 1610, when Galileo pointed his first primitive telescope at the starry host of heaven and said, "Wait! There are more stars than we had any idea!" Then came the 200-inch Mt. Palomar telescope, at that time the largest in the world, followed by NASA's Hubble Space Telescope, the renowned orbiting telescope. The discoveries made with these telescopes changed everything, and astronomers concluded that nobody really knows how many stars there are, but they estimate that there are more than 200 billion billion stars out there.

Got any idea how many 200 billion billion are? To help you grasp this, try this picture: There are over 7 billion people in the world. If every person in the world counted 50 billion stars, no two stars would be counted twice.

That's not the end, either. In a "try to top this one," Australian astronomers more recently panned strips of the starry sky in both the Canary Islands and in New South Wales (Australia). The team, working from the very powerful Anglo-Australian observatory in Australia, decided that there are about ten times as many stars in the sky as grains of sand on all the deserts and beaches of the world. That figure, so they estimate, is 70,000 million million million, or 70 sextillion! Dr. Simon Driver, who reported the findings to the General Assembly of the International Astronomical Union in Sydney, said there were likely many million more stars in the universe, but the figure of 70 sextillion was the number visible by modern telescopes.[71] Actually, the number of stars may be infinite. Who knows?

Who told Jeremiah that the stars were without number? Obviously, he didn't learn that from the scientific thought of his day. Nor did he learn that from the ancient astrologers. Jeremiah's insights could have come only from God. The Spirit of God gave witness to Jeremiah, who wrote truths and facts far beyond his times.

The Bible, surprisingly enough to some, mentions stars more than thirty times. It refers to some stars by precisely the same names as they are known today. Psalm 147:4 says that God counts the stars and calls them all by name.

One of the earliest dramas chronicled in Scripture is recorded in the Old Testament book of Job. This ancient writing says God made the Bear, Orion, and the Pleiades, and the constellations of the southern Zodiac, using the same names which astronomers use today (see Job 38:31). Psalm 33:6 says candidly, "By the word of the LORD the heavens were made." The next time you look towards heaven on a dark night and marvel at the starry hosts, start counting and remember the words of Jeremiah. He long ago made a point that science has since verified.

Are They Still Laughing at What Peter Wrote?

For centuries people read the following and couldn't comprehend what Peter was trying to say: "But the day of the Lord will come as a thief in the night, in which the heavens will pass away with a great noise, and the elements will melt with fervent heat; both the earth and the works that are in it will be burned up" (2 Peter 3:10 NKJV).

Obviously, Peter was speaking of Christ's Second Coming—an event that would be accompanied by cataclysmic disturbances in the atmosphere. He says the elements (*stoicheia,* meaning the materials comprising the planet) will melt with fervent heat. For centuries this seemed to be completely irreconcilable with anything educated men and women had learned, and sounded more like science fiction than biblical prophecy.

In 1867 the French scientist Pierre Vichelieu wrote in his diary, "The day will come when man will not only toy with the atom but will split an atom, and the energy of the sun itself shall be harnessed. When that day comes, God with his long beard will come down to earth and say, 'Gentlemen, it is time to close up shop.'" Less than a century later it happened! On a cold wintry day in December 1942, utilizing a squash court beneath the football field, a nuclear chain reaction was achieved as Enrico Fermi and his colleagues at the University of Chicago unleashed the power of nuclear fission. What took place that day enabled scientists to produce "Little Boy," the code name for the bomb that fell from a B-29 bomber, the *Enola Gay*, over the city of Hiroshima on August 6, 1945.

The bomb exploded in a yellow ball of fire that morphed into a mushroom-shaped cloud that rose to an altitude of 9,000 feet. Within minutes 80,000 people had died, and the final number of those killed or injured was twice that many. Yet all of the firepower of World War II, including the A-bombs dropped on Hiroshima and Nagasaki, equaled only 3 megatons of nuclear power. Three hundred megatons of nuclear power would destroy every major city in the world and create a colossal holocaust in the genre of the one that Peter described. But today, only God knows how many megatons of destructive nuclear power are available and could be unleashed in our world as the planet's "nuclear club" grows.

After the war, a news reporter standing at Hiroshima began his broadcast with these words, "I am standing at the spot where the end of the world began." In his famous position speech at Fulton, Missouri, Winston Churchill, who had led Britain through the war, said, "The Dark Ages may return on the gleaming wings of science—beware, I say, time may be short." With that horrible specter forever etched on the consciousness of the world, nobody now laughs at what Peter wrote. Suddenly those words have become a grave possibility.

What Did Moses Know That Sir William Harvey Proved?

Moses contended that the life of all flesh is in the blood (Leviticus 17:14). No one with medical knowledge, not even Hippocrates, the Greek father of medicine, would have agreed with Moses. It actually took science 3,000 years to catch up with that one. In 1628, Sir William Harvey discovered the principle of circulation. His contemporaries scoffed at him then, but he eventually proved his findings.

How did Moses know that the life of all flesh is in the blood if it was not that God revealed something to him which was eventually borne out by science? As the adopted son of an Egyptian princess, Moses' mindset and education should have reflected that of his Egyptian tutors, but it didn't. Moses' Egyptian contemporaries bathed in blood, thinking it would restore their vitality. Both cultured Romans and their pagan enemies thought that drinking blood—something forbidden in the Bible—would give them the physical strength of their enemies.

Remember seeing pictures of the old-fashioned barber pole outside barbershops? That barber pole originally meant that more than haircuts were given there. It was a sign indicating that "blood letting" was done on the premises—a practice that was believed to release the "bad blood," allowing healing to take place. History tells us that more than a few renowned individuals, including George Washington, might have lived longer had they not been victims of the well-meaning but ignorant practice of "blood letting." For centuries humankind knew that blood was significant but never understood what Moses wrote—that it is the source of life itself.

Does Color or Ethnicity Matter?

Two of the commodities in the world that control our lives are oil and blood. The price of a barrel of oil fluctuates depending on market supply and demand, whereas if blood were sold by the barrel it would cost about $20,000 for the same volume. (Here's some trivia: If all the blood that is donated annually in the world was collected—about 16 million gallons annually—it would fill thirty-two Olympic-sized swimming pools.)

When someone in an oil refinery makes a mistake and fuel is corrupted, cars may sputter and choke but nobody dies. However, if a mistake is made in a laboratory, the contamination may result in the large-scale loss of lives. For centuries, racial prejudice tainted our understanding of the nature of blood. Different nationalities were thought to have different kinds of blood. And because of attitudes of racial superiority, blood was neither universally donated nor received. Even in World War II, separate blood stocks were maintained from white and black donors for fear of offending people.

It was actually in 1900 that a Viennese doctor demonstrated conclusively that there are four major universal blood types which have nothing to do with racial heritage. Your color does not matter to God and never has! Addressing the philosophers and intellectuals of Athens, Paul declared, "And He has made from one blood[72] every nation of men to dwell on all the face of the earth, and has determined their preappointed times and the boundaries of their dwellings" (Acts 17:26 NKJV). Over 400 times, the Bible speaks of blood, elucidating its significance and underlining its importance to life and wholeness.

Is There Resolution to the Tension?

The great questions confronting us today involve our origin, purpose, and destiny, and it is the issue of purpose that will be the driving philosophical and religious issue of the twenty-first century. Nigel Brush, in his book *The Limitations of Scientific Truth*, aptly summarizes the impotence of science to speak to these pressing questions:

Only two answers have come to dominate the modern world. One is that humans were purposefully created by God in the past, are meant to serve him in the present, and have the opportunity to dwell with him forever in the future. The alternate answer states that random processes created humans, that we have no particular purpose in the present, and that we will cease to exist when we die.[73]

Surveys state that at least 80 percent of the population believes that humankind had a Creator and that design and purpose are evident in our world, leaving a scant 20 percent holding to the position that human existence and life on the planet is the result of random selection and change. Those who deny that humankind was created in the image of God struggle with the very concept of purpose—either in their personal lives or in history. The resolution of tension between science and religion involves both theology and philosophy.

The Bottom Line

Large numbers of qualified scientists in literally every field of science believe our world reflects creative design and that it did not "just happen." Some are quiet believers; others are outspoken in their faith, yet they are theistic. Many of them not only believe in God but acknowledge he sent his Son to bring redemption and healing to humankind.

While an entire book could be dedicated to this premise (some authors have done just that), the testimony of the German-born father of the US space program, Dr. Wernher von Braun, is exemplary and representative of those who are out of step with "political correctness," yet still adhere to a belief in God.

The historical library of NASA contains a copy of a letter written by von Braun dated January 3, 1972 in response to the inquiry of a Canadian woman asking if he believed in God. He replied,

> In my education, as I became exposed to the law and order of the universe, I was literally humbled by its unerring perfection. I became convinced that there must be Divine Intent behind it all. It is one thing to accept natural order as a way of life, but as I asked the question, "Why?" then God entered in all his glory. My experience with science led me to God.[74]

While it is unlikely that we will ever see a truce declared between science and religion, many individuals are quietly finding middle ground and declaring a private peace. One such person is Robert Jastrow, a renowned astronomer and physicist. Founding director of NASA's Goddard Institute for Space Studies, he is also the director of the Mount Wilson Institute and Hale Solar Laboratory. He has written the books *Red Giants and White Dwarfs* (1967) and *God and the Astronomers* (2nd ed., 2000). In an article written for the *New York Times* magazine, Jastrow concludes with this:

> For the scientist who has lived by his faith in the power of reason, the story ends like a bad dream. He has scaled the mountains of ignorance; he is about to conquer the highest peak; as he pulls himself over the final rock, he is greeted by a band of theologians who have been sitting there for centuries.[75]

> Who knows? I, for one, believe he is right.

CHAPTER 6

THE LIVING BOOK THAT CHANGES LIVES

When you read God's Word, you must constantly be saying to yourself, "It is talking to me, and about me."

Soren Kierkegaard[76]

In this chapter, you will meet five individuals whose lives have been transformed by the Bible, the book described by the writer of Hebrews as being "alive and active" (Hebrews 4:12).

Meet the Man Who Smoked Matthew, Mark, and Luke

Few people ever struck a stranger deal than did Gaylord Kambarami, the General Secretary of the Bible Society, who tried to sell a New Testament to a man in Zimbabwe. As Gaylord talked with the man, he could see he was interested. The stranger, however, was not interested in the content of the New Testament but was eyeing the size of the pages and the texture of the paper.

It was just the right size to use to roll his cigarettes. In fact, he told Gaylord that he wouldn't buy it, but if he gave it to him, he would take it and use the pages for cigarette paper.

"I understand that," Gaylord replied. "I will make a deal with you. I will give you this book if you promise to read every page before you smoke it." Pleased with himself that he indeed had the better end of the bargain, the man agreed to do so. Gaylord gave him the New Testament and the man walked away.

Years passed. Then one day Gaylord was attending a convention in Zimbabwe, when the speaker on the platform recognized him in the audience. Pointing to him excitedly, he said, "This man doesn't remember me, but I remember him." He explained, "About 15 years ago he tried to sell me a New Testament. When I refused to buy it he gave it to me, even though I told him I would use the pages to roll cigarettes." He continued this strange testimony, saying, "I smoked Matthew. I smoked Mark. Then I smoked Luke. But when I got to John 3, verse 16, I couldn't smoke any more. My life was changed from that moment!"

Now the former smoker is a full-time church evangelist devoting his life to showing others the way of salvation he found in this little book which had just the right size pages to roll cigarettes.

Strange, isn't it, how God honors the power of his Word to impact the lives of people! Paul Finkenbinder, known as Hermano Pablo in Latin America, tells the story of a man in El Salvador who discovered that the pages of a Bible were just the right size to wrap little purchases of produce at the market which he operated. He would rip a page or two from the book and wrap beans or rice for his customers. And when they got home and unwrapped their purchases, the villagers began reading the stories contained on this strange paper. Some of the people were keenly interested in what was happening. The stories were continued on the page of the next customer, so they began to compare pages, and through this strange method of evangelism people were converted and a church was born.

Unlike other books, the Bible is a living book. Long ago God promised Isaiah, "My word that goes out from my mouth . . . will not return to me empty, but will accomplish what I desire and achieve the purpose for which I sent it" (Isaiah 55:11).

Countless individuals have embarked on a "search and destroy mission" only to experience a life-changing encounter with this living book. Some have been intellectuals, some ordinary individuals, some historians, and through a diversity of different paths, they all ended up acknowledging that the Bible is no ordinary book.

Meet the Man Who Wrote the Story of My Favorite Movie

The 1959 movie *Ben Hur*, starring Charlton Heston, was one of the first Hollywood-produced movies I ever saw. The chariot race in that movie is one of Hollywood's finest hours, as Judah Ben Hur battles the cynical Messala, his one-time friend who has become his archrival and enemy.

But what makes the movie meaningful for me is the story behind the story. The film was based on a novel by General Lew Wallace, a man who served as a general in the American Civil War and later became governor of the State of Kansas. A friend of Wallace's, Robert Ingersoll, who was an outspoken agnostic, challenged Wallace to write a book debunking the myth of Jesus as recorded in the Bible and picture him as Ingersoll believed he was—an ordinary man no different from any of us.

Wallace took the challenge, but he was quickly confronted with the fact that he knew practically nothing about Jesus Christ, so he decided to research the subject before he started writing. And where do you find biographies of Jesus' life but in the New Testament? The more he studied, the more Wallace became convinced that Jesus was the person he claimed to be, and thus he wrote the book *Ben Hur: A Tale of the Christ*, a story that represents the testimony of his own changed life as a result of his study of the Bible.

Meet the Agnostic Doctor Who Knew He Could Debunk the Bible

Viggo Olsen's resumé reads like a "Who's Who" in medicine and includes details about his professional honors, international recognition, and credit for establishing a hospital in southern Bangladesh, where modern medical care was previously unknown. Recognizing him for his work with the people of Bangladesh, the Ambassador declared him to be "a true friend of Bangladesh" and honored him with visa #001 "in recognition of [his] service to our country."

The remarkable story of what Dr. Viggo Olsen accomplished is written in an award-winning book *Daktar/ Diplomat in Bangladesh* and in *Daktar II*. Should you have had the opportunity of meeting Dr. Olsen, as I once did, you would never think that this rather quiet, self-effacing gentleman with graying hair and expressive eyes once set out to discredit Scripture, to prove that it is not only unscientific but irrational and full of errors—historically, scientifically, and logically.

Dr. Olsen tells the story of his encounter with the truth in an autobiographical book entitled *The Agnostic Who Cared to Search*. It wasn't that Olsen cunningly set himself against generations of believers. He simply could not believe that educated men and women living in an era of enlightenment and scientific advancement could believe some of the preposterous-sounding things recorded in the Bible.

Olsen's challenge to the credibility of the Bible was the result of the irritation caused by his wife's parents. They were committed Christians who shared their faith by letters, pamphlets, and newspaper clippings with pointed comments from a Christian perspective—most of which were immediately trashed. But it was when Viggo and Joan visited her parents' home that the encounters grew more heated, more intense, and more challenging.

After a debate over Christianity that lasted until two a.m., Viggo and his wife agreed to look at the business of God and faith, and make a reasoned decision as to why they were rejecting the whole thing as an outmoded and leftover practice from a bygone era. Olsen said, "We would prove the Bible is not the Word of God, that Christianity is *not* the true religion of God, and that Christ was but a man, *not* the Son of God."[77]

Their starting point was to survey all of the arguments against God he had heard and believed during his years of study—God is invisible, all roads lead to God (if there is one), and the touchstone issue of suffering, thereby proving God's disinterest and weakness in what happens to humankind.

Part of the agreement they made with Joan's parents was that during this "search-and-destroy mission" they would attend church—something which, at times, made them very uncomfortable.

In his study, Olsen stumbled across a book by Dr. Henry Morris (mentioned in the previous chapter), a top-notch scientist with ample credentials, and read other publications written by scientists who believed in God and the record of Scripture. Slowly the Olsens' airtight logic began to develop some hairline cracks. Gradually, the balance tilted as it made more sense to accept the historical record and to believe than to disbelieve.

Then unexpectedly, Olsen's world took a hit! His wife gave birth prematurely to an infant baby boy—the "spitting image" of his father—who lived for only forty hours, then died. Seeing others die is one thing; seeing your firstborn son die is entirely another matter.

Something struck Olsen: He loved this tiny baby, who was his own flesh and blood. Then he began thinking of the Father who also gave his Son, who died outside the walls of Jerusalem. By this time, Olsen had accepted the historical record that Jesus did live and die, and that God does love us and wanted to communicate that love to us through his Son. "If I could love an infant son who looked like me," he wrote, "how much the Father must have loved his Son so much like him. My very human love focused on a tiny son I didn't even know; God's love—infinite, divine—enfolded a Son whom he had known for eternity."[78]

When tragedy strikes, you either turn to the Lord or turn against him, and Viggo and Joan Olsen took refuge in him who not only loves us but comforts us in our times of sorrow. The Olsens never turned back, and the agnostic who dared to search redirected his life and energies into making a significant difference in our world.

Meet the Apostle to the Agnostics

He is known simply as C. S. Lewis. When he died on November 22, 1963, most newspapers never mentioned that fact. Some papers carried a brief news note on an inside page, stating that the Cambridge Professor of Medieval Literature had died of heart and kidney failure. On page one of newspapers on the day Lewis died was the vivid picture of an American president, John F. Kennedy, who had been cut down by an assassin's bullets. No wonder Lewis's passing drew only scant mention.

His full name was Clive Staples Lewis, which may account for his using only the initials "C. S." or simply the name "Jack" with his personal friends. Lewis was a brilliant man and a keen thinker. He wrote on a vast number of themes, including English literature, theology, and children's stories such as the The Chronicles of Narnia, filled with mythical beings and fairy tale characters.

The cover of a *Time* magazine featured Lewis, dubbing him "Apostle to the Agnostics." Some refer to Lewis as an apologist, or one who defends Christianity, yet Lewis never really intended to defend anything. His book *Mere Christianity*, which came from a series of radio lectures broadcast during World War II, was the tool that brought Chuck Colson, known as "Richard Nixon's hatchet man," to an understanding of who Jesus Christ is. After his conversion, Colson spoke to the hearts of millions of people. His logical, intuitive mind simply concluded that it is more rational to accept the gospel and its implications than to disbelieve it.

As a youth, Lewis was a believer. Then, partly because of the death of his mother and his experiences in World War I, he abandoned his faith and claimed to be an atheist. Eventually, however, the gospel again became meaningful to him, and he fully embraced Christianity, this time with commitment.

Lewis never based his salvation on feelings or emotional experiences. To the contrary, he later wrote that before he was converted there were times when Christianity seemed very logical, and after his conversion there were times when atheism also seemed logical. He believed that you have to tell your emotions where to get off; otherwise, you dither back and forth, uncertain of who you are or what you believe.

His personal life was complex and his path to faith was marked by intense struggles and personal conflicts. He never learned to drive a car and he was a failure when it came to practical things like fixing something around the house. Though book royalties eventually amounted to large sums, he generously gave most of it away and never could handle money well. But he was a master at handling words. When it came to making complex things simple, he was good—very, very good.

Lewis met Joy Gresham, an American writer who admired him. He eventually married her and became a father to her two children. When they were first getting acquainted, Lewis was attracted to Joy but didn't really love her. Forced, however, with either the choice of marrying her or losing her because the British government was going to deport her, he married her. He eventually fell deeply in love with Joy, and she became an indispensable part of his life.

When she died of cancer, Lewis was shattered. He felt as though God let him down. "I turn to God now that I really need him," said Lewis, "and what do I find? A door slammed in my face, the sound of bolting and double-bolting, and after that . . . silence."[79] Yet Lewis held on to his faith, not based on his feelings of pain and loss. If there is one very powerful thing about which the life of C. S. Lewis speaks to my heart, it is that faith must never be based on our emotions but on the truth of the gospel, which rises above sensations or feelings. It was the Bible that became his bridge from skepticism and doubt to faith and commitment.

Meet the Schoolteacher Who Had to Know the Truth for Himself

You may have never heard of the little village of Chuguyevka in the Russian Far East, some 350 kilometers from Vladivostok, and I wouldn't be surprised. How I found myself in this remote village where strangers must register with the police and having a refrigerator is the exception rather than the rule is part of the remarkable story behind the conversion of Genya Gvozdenko, a man who, having grown up under Communism and never held a Bible in his hands, was eventually changed by the power of the Bible.

Genya, along with his wife Lyena and children, was living in the distant Russian province of Prymorye, where he taught school and spent his spare time working in his garden. Then one day, shortly after Perestroika began to change the face of Communism, Genya went to market and noticed someone with a display of Bibles laid out on a rickety table. Although he had heard about the Bible, he had never seen one. Curious, he picked up one and looked through it. He knew that under Communism it had been impossible to buy a Bible even if you had money for one—which this poor schoolteacher did not.

Seeing that he was interested in the book, the missionary who displayed the Bibles agreed to let the schoolteacher take one home if he returned it the next day. Genya showed the book to his wife, then sat down and started reading. He read all night, and by the time daylight had pierced the eastern sky, the light of God's love had penetrated his heart. He decided then that he wanted to know more about God.

Returning the next day, Genya asked the missionary where he could learn more about this book and the God who says he loves us. The missionary told him about a fledgling new Christian school in Donetsk, Ukraine. Now, if you drew a straight line between Chuguyevka and Donetsk, you would note that it stretches across eleven time zones and thousands of miles across the vast expanse of the former Soviet Union. Making the decision to go to the Christian school, Genya quit his job, sold his cow, and bought train tickets for the long journey, which took eight days and nights.

Upon finally arriving in Donetsk, the family made their way to the school, which had not received their application and so did not expect the schoolteacher and his family. But they could hardly send them back, so they accepted Genya as a student. That's where I met the Gvozdenkos and was impressed by their sincerity and commitment to the cause of Jesus Christ. Now, having completed his training, Genya and his family have returned to the remote area in the Far East and have planted an evangelical church.

Is theirs an easy task? No way. I've been there and know what they are up against. First, there is the physical difficulty. Would you care to raise five children in a log house consisting of three rooms? Thirty meters from the house is a pipe coming out of the ground, a faucet attached, with cold water—when the pipe is not frozen. A broken mirror is attached to the wall of the cooking house, which also serves as a bath house, and behind this is a little shack with no modern plumbing. In the winter temperatures dip below minus fifty degrees centigrade, and the snow can be a meter deep.

Are Genya and Lyena discouraged? Not for a moment. They are positive and upbeat, pleased that they have planted a church where needs are so great. The two-edged sword of God's Word still cuts through the gloom of our old world, bringing hope and life.

The Bottom Line

The impact of the Bible in changing the lives of people for the better is unrivaled. Have you ever heard anyone say, "When I began reading books on science and technology, my heart was strangely drawn towards God"? Or, "When I began studying philosophy and history, I was converted and gave my life for Christian service"?

When a newspaper asked people, "What is the most impressive book you have ever read?" the Bible was mentioned more than any other book. One person responded, "My life and my seven-year-old son's life were forever changed when someone gave me a Bible in a translation I could understand."

Another gave this testimony:

The Bible remained on my bookshelf gathering dust while I had feelings of guilt for not reading it. I'm still not sure why I picked it up one day and began seriously reading it. I remember thinking that if Christians were right about Jesus, I had better know what God was saying to me. . . . My intent was to read it for intellectual purposes, but something happened that day and to my surprise I began to understand the words with my heart and spirit. That was the beginning of a very different life for me.[80]

If you have never made a serious study of this book that tells you how to connect with God, better get started. It can make the difference between spiritual survival and failure when the winds of adversity blow and the dark winter of trouble begins to engulf you. The writer of Hebrews describes his confidence that God will honor his Word as "an anchor for the soul, firm and secure" (Hebrews 6:19).

Accepting what the Bible says isn't a matter of trying to convince yourself to believe something that isn't true. It is acknowledging the historical record of what God tells us about life, about his love and his concern for us. Not knowing this is an ignorance you can ill afford.

There is great comfort in knowing that the promises of God's Word have your name attached to them, so when you face the inevitable troubles and difficulties of living in a broken world, you know God is not indifferent to your needs but will see you through. This assurance is found only in the Bible. A stanza from "No Other Plea," a nineteenth-century hymn with words written by Lidie H. Edmunds, puts it so well:

> My heart is leaning on the Word,
> the written Word of God,
>
> Salvation by my Savior's name,
> salvation through His blood.
>
> I need no other argument,
> I need no other plea;
>
> It is enough that Jesus died,
> and that He died for me.

CHAPTER 7

THE IMPLICATIONS OF UNCERTAINTY

The deathless book has survived three great dangers:
the neglect of its friends; the false systems built upon it;
the warfare of those who hated it.

Isaac Taylor[81]

In 1911, thieves broke into the world's most prestigious art gallery, the Louvre, in Paris, and took the most famous painting in the history of art: Leonardo da Vinci's *Mona Lisa*. It can never be said that the thieves did not have good taste. During the two-year period when the haunting image of the woman with the semi-smile was missing, more people came to the gallery to stare at the empty spot on the wall than had gone to look at the masterpiece in the previous twelve years. Think about it! People were going to see *what wasn't there*!

It is only when there is a blank spot on the wall of our lives that we begin to realize the value of what is missing—something that is precious and meaningful to those who have been denied what we take for granted. The empty place speaks loudly and clearly.

For many—perhaps you as well—that blank spot on the wall of your life has resulted in uncertainty, a lack of definition as to who you are, where you are going, and what your life is all about. C. S. Lewis once used the analogy of a ship on the ocean and he said that three questions have to be faced: First, how do you keep the ship from sinking? Then, how do you keep it from running into other ships? But more important, why is it out there at all?

The answer to what your life is about will never be found through the study of science or philosophy, but in this book that is a reliable bridge across the dark chasm of uncertainty that obscures the future.

By now, you have walked with me across a number of bridges. This evidence is what has led me to have confidence that the Bible is what it claims to be: the Word of God. The Bible's uniqueness, the manuscript evidence, fulfilled prophecy, the findings of archaeology and science, and the lives of people who have been changed by this book all point to its writing being more than human endeavor could have accomplished, and therefore, of supreme importance. Reading the Bible causes you to conclude, "Yes, God said that!"

Some truths are so profound and meaningful that it becomes intensely painful to confront them. Furthermore, embracing them at times requires changes in our lifestyles that we don't want to make, so we tend to look the other way or give feeble intellectual assent to truth apart from a commitment to its direction.

On one occasion Peter came to Jesus and asked, "Lord, to whom shall we go? You have the words of eternal life" (John 6:68). That yearning or passion to know God and commune with him often lies dormant in our hearts and lives. Yes, we believe, at least theoretically, that the Bible is God's Word and confirm that belief by adding new editions and translations to our overburdened shelves. But—and here is where the whole equation turns the corner—we often feel that our duties are complete by acknowledging those beliefs and making token commitments to them.

However, when people choose to ignore what a map or compass says, preferring to rely on their feelings, they may well be in for a rough ride. The Bible is not only cross-cultural in the sense that it embraces all humankind, but is also cross-cultural in that it provides a clear understanding of right and wrong, often rejecting practices that are socially acceptable today. It postulates moral absolutes that are as unchanging as the North Star, the same regardless of the weather or the vagaries of human opinion. It tells you who God is, who you are, and how you can get through life without falling on your face.

"Just a minute," you may be thinking. "Does it really matter that much what my views are of this book?" If the Bible is true, it matters tremendously. You then have four options.

Confronting the Truth of the Bible

OPTION 1: You Can Ignore the Bible and What It Says

I often think of the instruction manual for a small single-engine aircraft that says something like this: "If you are flying at night and you lose power, try to restart the engine. If that fails, when you reach an altitude of 200 meters, turn on your landing lights. If you don't like what you see, then turn them off again."

The sad fact is that a lot of people have turned off their landing lights when it comes to very important things. Some do it in a high school or college classroom. Some do it simply because they don't like what the Bible says—too confining, too limiting, too puritanical. They like what they are doing and don't want to change, so they just "turn off the lights."

Actually, that is what vast numbers of people do, many of whom even go to church every Sunday, have a half-dozen or more Bibles in their homes, and support humanitarian causes. That's about as far as their faith really takes them.

At times the neglect of the personal encouragement and direction that the Bible gives is nothing less than tragic. Dick Johnson was serving as a police chaplain for the Urbandale-Des Moines Police Force when he received an urgent summons to report to a home where there had been a disturbance. Dick is often called upon to provide counseling, help, encouragement, and support when it is needed. For one couple, however, his help was too little and too late. A husband had become jealous over the attention that his wife had been giving to a mutual friend. Pointing a gun at the head of his wife, asleep on the sofa, he pulled the trigger, then took his own life as well—a murder-suicide.

As Dick came into the living room, the scene of the crime, he noticed that a Bible was lying two feet from the head of the woman who had become the victim. He picked it up. It was a confirmation Bible that had been presented to the husband when he had finished his religious instruction and had become a church member.

"The answer to their problems," said Dick, "was there, only twenty-four inches away. In that book was the solution to their conflict and all of their anger and frustrations. The answer was so close physically, yet ignored."

OPTION 2: You Can Trivialize the Bible

You can reduce it to the level of good literature and nothing more. Many people, having never read or studied the Bible, mock or scorn the book as a collection of myths and fables, making light of anyone who takes the Bible seriously. Thousands of young adults, having grown up in a Christian home, having gone to Sunday school as youngsters, hit college campuses and suddenly find that anyone who actually believes the Bible is considered an "intellectual throwback," a kind of weird non-conformist, who has no real academic future.

OPTION 3: You Can Flat-Out Deny the Truth of the Bible

You then are faced with the task of explaining how the Bible has been the inspiration for the world's greatest literature, art, and music down through the centuries. You are forced to offer psychological explanations for the life-changing conversion experiences of people who say, "Reading that book changed my life!" You can interpret and explain the influence of the Bible however you wish, yet the fact remains that denying something doesn't change the consequences of truth, no matter how you choose to ignore it.

I once had an unexpected encounter as I sat down in a restaurant across the aisle from two men who were engaged in a rather heated discussion. Attempting to mind my own business, I began reading the menu, but it was impossible for me not to overhear their conversation. It went something like this: "You call yourself a Christian? Why do you believe in Jesus Christ?"

The friend having lunch with the interrogator hadn't expected the inquisition. He hesitated, then responded, "I believe that he died for me and that his death took away my sin."

"How do you know that Christ ever lived anyway?"

"Because the Bible says so." And that settled the issue—right? Not exactly.

The antagonist launched a rather loud and caustic oration, stating that the Bible was a collection of myths and fables that came out of the superstitious Middle Ages, and if God existed at all we could not know him. Then he said, "Besides this, all religious faith is based on 'what men think'—not facts."

At this point the conversation was a great deal more interesting than the list of soup and sandwiches on the menu in front of me so I spoke up. "Please excuse me for interrupting your conversation, but I couldn't help overhearing, and what you have said is of interest to me. Would you mind if I asked a question?" Both said, "Certainly not."

Then, turning to the fellow who was quite certain that his friend had been deceived by Christianity, I asked, "Suppose that your friend, who is a Christian, is entirely wrong. Suppose that there really was no such person called Jesus Christ and that the Bible is a fraud—not God's revelation to humankind at all. Let's suppose that life ends when you die—that's it, and there is no heaven or hell and no life hereafter. Now suppose this is true, what has this fellow lost?"

He answered, "I suppose that he has not lost anything, because he believed in something that did not exist."

Then I said, "On the other hand, suppose he is right, suppose that there is a heaven, a hell, and a God, and that he sent his Son to pay the price of our sin and give us eternal life, what have you lost?"

He sat in stunned silence for a moment and then blurted out, "Well, that is not the question, but I never thought of it like that."

OPTION 4: You Can Embrace the Bible and What It Teaches

The implications of the contents of the Bible are tremendous, touching every part of my life, including my business, my marriage, my money, my ethics, my work, my morality, my sex life, my views of men and women, how I treat the elderly, what I think about abortion and stem-cell research, and on and on.

The greater your knowledge of this book, the greater will be your respect for it, and when you come to understand that it is a book given by God, you gradually begin to recognize that God gave us his direction for our benefit, not to make us miserable, but to show us how to live.

The inertia separating the widely-held beliefs of people today and the counsel of the Bible can be overcome by persuasion that is stronger than our indifference and our neglect. Ben Johnson, the seventeenth-century poet, once said that the prospect of being hanged "wonderfully concentrates the mind," and so does a challenge to your security or future.

For Viggo Olsen it was the death of a child. For some it is a divorce and the loneliness that follows. The somber words of a doctor, "I am sorry to tell you that you have an inoperable cancer," suddenly make a person search for something to dispel fears and provide security. For others it is simply the quiet persuasion of the Holy Spirit speaking to your heart saying, "This is the way, walk in it!" If you are now convinced about what the Bible truly is, then what? What are the steps you can do to fully embrace the truth of Scripture?

Embracing the Truth of the Bible

STEP 1: Make a Commitment of Faith

Act upon the evidence that I have discussed in the various chapters of this book. The Archbishop of Canterbury once said that "the longest journey in the life of one's belief is from the head to the heart."[82] With your intellect you acknowledge truth but with your heart you appropriate that truth.

Trusting what the Bible says requires a commitment— not a blind faith but one based on evidence that dispels uncertainty and hesitancy. Apart from it, your faith will surely falter. W. H. Murray,[83] one of the team members of the 1951 Scottish Himalayan Expedition, in an often-quoted statement about the importance of commitment, wrote,

> Until one is committed, there is hesitancy, the chance to draw back, always ineffectiveness. Concerning all acts of initiative (and creation), there is one elementary truth, the ignorance of which kills countless ideas and splendid plans: that the moment one definitely commits oneself, then Providence moves too. All sorts of things occur to help one that never would have otherwise occurred. A whole stream of events issues from the decision, raising in one's favor all manner of unforeseen incidents and meetings and material assistance, which no man could have dreamt would have come his way.[84]

It was commitment that Joshua had in mind when he challenged his hearers,

> "But if serving the LORD seems undesirable to you, then choose for yourselves this day whom you will serve, whether the gods your ancestors served beyond the Euphrates, or the gods of the Amorites, in whose land you are living. But as for me and my household, we will serve the LORD." (Joshua 24:15)

STEP 2: Live Up to the Knowledge You Have

Quite often what we do not understand doesn't bother us nearly as much as what we do understand. Frankly, that's what growing in the grace and knowledge of the Lord Jesus Christ (2 Peter 3:18) is about. You may not understand everything. Nobody does. But when the Holy Spirit gives you enlightenment as to what he wants you to do, you need the courage to say, "Yes, Lord, yes, I will."

STEP 3: Strive to Know the Truth That Will Set You Free

That's what Jesus told the disciples in John 8:32. But the truth is divisive, and the only way you can be sure that your persuasions are right is when you have confidence that the Bible is trustworthy. The harsh reality is that today we are in a cultural and spiritual war that will repeatedly put you, if you are a believer, at odds with our society and force you to swim upstream.

C. S. Lewis contended that you need to know what a straight line is before you know what a crooked one is, and, like it or not, the truth of this book is the straight line that says, "Do this!" and "Don't do that!" It has the same ring of authority that a guide who knows the jungle has when he speaks to a lost traveler, telling him how to come out safely on the other side. The negatives of this book are not to inhibit you or keep you from finding happiness but to guide you through the hazards of life.

But once you close the door on lifestyles that, of necessity, reject the position that the Bible is true, you draw a line in the sand and take a rather narrow path—one trod by countless of pilgrims and sojourners who like Moses of old "chose to be mistreated along with the people of God rather than to enjoy the fleeting pleasures of sin" (Hebrews 11:25).

Long ago Jesus said that a commitment to truth and uprightness would result in schism. He told the disciples,

> "Do not suppose that I have come to bring peace to the earth. I did not come to bring peace, but a sword. For I have come to turn 'a man against his father, a daughter against her mother, a daughter-in-law against her mother-in-law—a man's enemies will be the members of his own household.'" (Matthew 10:34-36)

The key to knowing that God's Word is truth is a desire to do what God wants you to do. If you really have a desire to know God's will for your life—if you truly want to do the right thing, God will reveal to you that his Word is true. Jesus promised, "Anyone who chooses to do the will of God will find out whether my teaching comes from God or whether I speak on my own" (John 7:17). Strive to obey what you read in the Bible, and you will discern that it is, indeed, a living book.

STEP 4: Realize That Obedience Brings Blessing and Disobedience Brings Consequences

Once you settle the issue that the Bible is trustworthy and reliable and the counsel it gives comes from the heart of a loving Father who knows what is best for his children, you then confront the reality that God meant what the writers of Scripture penned long ago. But—and this is important—committing to his will and purpose for your life not only relieves you of a great burden but brings his blessing as well.

The first chapter of the book of Psalms begins with the promise of reward, saying, "Blessed is the man who does not walk in the counsel of the wicked or stand in the way of sinners or sit in the seat of mockers." Frankly, some words are difficult to understand in the cultural context of life today. Such is the word "blessed." Check out synonyms for the word and you will find the word "happy," but the Hebrew word that the writer used some 3,000 years ago encompassed far more than the state of mind we describe as being "happy." It includes the concepts of wholeness, completeness, and a sense of well-being that is often sought today but seldom found in a world that puts far more importance on what we have than what we are.

Jesus stressed the importance of *doing* as opposed to *hearing and sampling.* "Why do you call me, 'Lord, Lord,'" he asked, "and do not do what I say?" (Luke 6:46). On another occasion he used the analogy of two individuals who built houses—one on sand, the other on rock (a firm foundation)—to contrast those who embrace the truth and those who have no foundation for their lives. Then he went to the bottom line: "The one who hears my words and does not put them into practice is like a man who built a house on the ground without a foundation. The moment the torrent struck that house, it collapsed and its destruction was complete" (Luke 6:49).

James, the half-brother of Jesus, writing one of the first New Testament documents, said, "Do not merely listen to the word, and so deceive yourselves. Do what it says" (James 1:22). He puts the emphasis on commitment and motivation to positive action—not merely "listening" or "hearing" the Word. This was the same emphasis Paul made in his landmark letter to the Romans. "It is not those who hear the law," he said, "who are righteous in God's sight, but it is those who obey the law who will be declared righteous" (Romans 2:13).

Once you realize Jesus Christ did not come to condemn the world but that the world through him might be saved (John 3:17), matters embracing the supernatural are no longer stumbling blocks, barricading you from crossing the bridge of confidence to what the Bible says.

The questions confronting us are profound but simple;

- Is there a God?

- What kind of a God is he?

- Has he communicated with us expressing his love, his purpose, and his will through the Bible?

This book specifically deals with the last question, and when you answer that in the affirmative, you have discovered what David did long ago, that God's Word is "a lamp for my feet, a light on my path" (Psalm 119:105). And then you will hear a quiet but powerful voice say, "Whether you turn to the right or to the left, your ears will hear a voice behind you, saying, 'This is the way; walk in it'" (Isaiah 30:21).

What more can you ask for?

GETTING STARTED
IN STUDYING THE BIBLE

You have only ten minutes before you head for the kitchen in the morning. After that you're off to work, come home tired at the end of the day, fix supper for your family or think about getting through the file in your briefcase, and then fall exhausted into bed. Your conscience nags at you a bit, and you really want to pick up your Bible and spend a few minutes in the Word. "Can I really get anything out of this in just ten minutes?" you ask yourself as you debate even bothering to pick up your Bible. The following guidelines will help you get started:

Guideline 1: Concentration

As you sit down and let your Bible fall open, your first battle is with your thoughts that flood your mind and wage war with your concentration. Shut out the rest of the day and the tyranny of pressing obligations to the extent that you can and focus on what you are reading. Then, expect God to speak to you. The depth of your encounter with the Word—connecting with God's direction and will for your day—is far more important than how many chapters or pages your eyes quickly scan without comprehending what you are reading.

Guideline 2: Observation

You need to observe what you are reading and understand it to profit from it, right? I am amazed at times that I can read a page, close the book and not remember one thing that I read. Like the seed that falls on the wayside, the vultures of my schedule have plucked it out of my memory. My mind has been racing on to the day's agenda or the problems I'm dealing with instead of concentrating on those moments with the Word.

A one-volume commentary such as Wycliffe's Bible Commentary or *Halley's Bible Handbook* provides concise, focused help. Today there are many study Bibles with reference notes that are helpful and illuminating—well worth the additional cost. If the Bible is new to you, I suggest that you start with the gospel of John, and then go on to the book of Acts, to get a comprehensive grasp of the whole. No matter what you do, however, do not ignore the Old Testament, which is the cradle of the New, and is all part and parcel of the book.

Guideline 3: Interpretation

What does it mean? Generally, the clearest, simplest interpretation is the correct one. Some would have you to think that only those with great spiritual insights can interpret the Bible. When I hear someone trying to convince an audience that he has "insights" which others have not been spiritual enough to gain, I usually catalog the speaker as a sensationalist. God did not give his Word to PhD holders but to common, ordinary people, and common, ordinary meanings are usually right on target.

Guideline 4: Application

How do I apply this great truth to my life? Most of what the Bible says is pretty much "plain vanilla." God's purpose in giving us this magnificent book is to help us know how to live. Right living, God's plan, his blueprint—all of these are revealed in the Bible. As you apply to your life what you read each day, the Bible will become a living book to you.

ENDNOTES

CHAPTER 1:
The Uniqueness of the Bible

1   http://www.time.com/time/covers/0,16641,19311214,00.html

2   Neil Lightfoot, *How We Got the Bible* (Grand Rapids: Baker, 2005), 12.

3   Pliny, a first-century Roman historian and educator, said that civilization was dependent upon on the use of papyrus. For a thorough discussion of papyrus and its development see Lightfoot's *How We Got the Bible*, 17-19.

4   The Greek word, *biblia*, which gives us the English word "book" referred to the papyrus manuscripts made from the papyrus reed grown on the banks of the Nile.

5   Much of what was commonly believed in Egypt in the fourteenth century before Christ was in direct conflict with what Moses recorded in the book of Genesis. Moses wrote, "In the beginning God created the heavens and the earth," but common wisdom was that the earth was hatched from an egg and that symbol adorns sarcophagi and monuments of that era. Luke explains: "Moses was educated in all the wisdom of the Egyptians and was powerful in speech and action" (Acts 7:22).

6   Norman L. Geisler and William E. Nix, *From God to Us* (Chicago: Moody Press, 1974), 13.

7   Erwin W. Lutzer, *You Can Trust The Bible* (Chicago: Moody Press, 1998), 38.

8   In 1863, a Richard Roethe theorized that *Koine* Greek was a new "language of the Holy Ghost." That premise was

widely accepted until Adolf Deissmann, a German pastor and scholar, analyzed the Greek text of various reading in the papyri, comparing it with the Greek text of the New Testament and discovered that there were many similarities, thus demonstrating that the Greek of the New Testament was only ordinary Greek spoken commonly through out the world. Norman Geisler and William Nix explain, "Until the late nineteenth century, New Testament Greek was believed to be a special 'Holy Ghost' language, but since that time it has come to be identified as one of the five states of development of Greek itself. This *Koine* Greek was the most widely known language throughout the world of the first century." Geisler and Nix, *From God to Us*, 129.

9   Geisler and Nix, *From God to Us*, 8.

10   Phillip Yancey, "The Bible Jesus Read," *Christianity Today*, January 11, 1999, 67.

11   While Hebrew Bibles contain 24 books, they consist of the same 39 books found in English Bibles. The Hebrew Scriptures combine some books generally making three sections: the law, the writings, and the prophets.

12   Ravi Zacharias, *Walking from East to West* (Grand Rapids: Zondervan, 2006), 176.

13   According to the German scholar Adolph Deissman, the oldest use of the Greek word translated "Gospel" *euangelion* was an inscription on an Greek stone telling how two armies had met in combat, and one was victorious, and a runner was dispatched to the city with the *euangelion* or good news of the victory.

14   The dates that I am providing in this chapter are generally advanced by conservative theologians such as Henry Clarence Thiessen in his benchmark *Introduction to the New Testament* (Peabody, MA: Hendrickson Publishers: 2002).

15 Lightfoot, *How We Got the Bible*, 203.

16 Ravi Zacharias, *Can Man Live Without God?* (Waco, TX: Word, 1994), xviii.

17 C. S. Lewis, *Mere Christianity* (New York: Macmillan, 1969), 45.

CHAPTER 2:
The Powerful Testimony of Manuscript Evidence

18 Norman L. Geisler, personal correspondence dated December 1, 2006.

19 Nigel Gillingham in *Qumran*, a pictorial guide, says, "A group of Bedouin from the Ta'amireh tribe were on their way from Transjordan to the black market in Bethlehem. The purpose of the journey was to sell a herd of 'contraband' goats. Normally such a route would not have been used but due to the political scene in Palestine at that time, before the birth of the State of Israel, they needed a route that would avoid both British and Arab patrols. It was on this journey through the Judean Wilderness that the discovery took place" (Herzila, Israel: Palphot Marketing Ltd, n.d.), 4.

20 John Trever was the first to photograph the scroll in its original condition. In their book *The Meaning of the Dead Sea Scrolls* authors James VanderKam and Peter Flint says Trever's *The Untold Story of Qumran* provides the best and most comprehensive account of the initial discovery. In a footnote, they say that Trever refers to numerous tape-recorded interviews with the Bedouins who responded to 63 questions he put to them. Their answers, of course, comply with the "lost goat" story.

21 Harry Thomas Frank, *Understanding the Dead Sea Scrolls*, edited by Hershel Shanks (New York: Random House, 1992), 5–6.

22   Ibid., 6.

23   Eleazar L. Sukenik as quoted by Moshe Pearlman in *The Dead Sea Scrolls in the Shrine of the Book* (Tel Aviv: 1999), 14.

24   Prior to the discovery of the Isaiah manuscripts, the Nash Papyrus, containing among other things The Ten Commandments from Deuteronomy 5, dating to the second or first century B.C. was considered to be the oldest portions of the Old Testament at that time.

25   Author's personal interview with Mrs. Elizabeth Trever on January 9, 2007 in Lake Forest, California.

26   The Dead Sea Scrolls," http://www.crystalinks.com/dss.html.

27   http://www.jewishvirtuallibrary.org/jsource/History/deadsea.html.

28   Howard F. Vos, *Beginnings in Bible Archaeology* (Chicago: Moody Press, 1971), 54.

29   Frederic Kenyon, *Handbook to the Textual Criticism of the New Testament* (New York: Macmillan, 1912), 5.

30   Frederic Kenyon, *The Bible and Archaeology* (New York: Harper, 1940), 288.

31   C. Tischendorf, *Codex Sinaiticus: The Ancient Biblical Manuscript Now in the British Museum: Tischendorf's Story and Argument Related by Himself*, 8th ed. (London: Butterworth Press, 1933), 16–17.

32   Ibid.

33   L. Schneller, *Search on Sinai: The Story of Tischendorf's Life and the Search for a Lost Manuscript*, trans. Dorothee Schroeder (London: Epworth, 1939), 71.

34   Upon the death of Voltaire the Geneva Bible society purchased his old home and upon Voltaire's own press printed a complete edition of the Bible.

35 Bruce Metzger in his seminal *The Text of the New Testament* says, "[The Sinai Manuscript] is the oldest complete manuscript of the entire Bible. . . ." He says Sinaiticus "once contained the entire Bible. . . . Today parts of the Old Testament have perished, but . . . the entire New Testament has survived . . . the only known complete copy of the Greek New Testament in uncial script." (p. 42).

36 While the Vatican dates this manuscript at about 325 AD, other scholars, such as Gordon Fee, date the manuscript at about 350 AD; however, all are in general agreement that it is dated about the middle of the fourth century. Bruce Metzger says that "the complete absence of ornamentation from Vaticanus has generally been taken as an indication that it is slightly older than codex Sinaiticus" (Metzger, *The Text of the New Testament*, 47).

37 Consider the fact that the average manuscript would consist of about 30 leaves or sheets, and since an animal's hide would provide for about two sheets, the hides of at least 15 animals would be required.

38 See 1 Corinthians 2:7–13; 14:37; 1 Thessalonians 2:13.

39 Lightfoot, *How We Got the Bible*, 157.

CHAPTER 3:

The Contribution of Archaeology

40 Nelson Glueck, *Rivers in the Desert*, as quoted by Richard De Haan in *The Book You Can Trust* (Grand Rapids: RBC Publications, n.d.), 7.

41 Jeffery Sheler, "Mysteries of the Bible," *U.S. News and World Report*, April 17, 1995, 62.

42 In one of his books on Christian evidence, Harry Rimmer called attention to the fact that the historical books of the Old

Testament record the names of 47 kings in addition to those kings who reigned in Israel and Judah. As great as some of these men were, they were completely forgotten by posterity, and for some 2,300 years their names were unknown to secular scholars. Most secular historians relegated their existence to mythology and considered their exploits as myths. "Now," says Guy P. Duffield, "all 47 of them have been transferred from the columns of mythology to the accepted records of established history."

43 Jeffery Sheler, "Mysteries of the Bible," 64.

44 "Geographica," *National Geographic*, January 1992, 20.

45 Following Garstang's work the British archaeologist Kathleen Kenyon broke with Garstang's findings, holding to a later date for the destruction of Jericho. At this point the ruins have been so sacked that it is impossible to determine exactly what happened and when it took place.

46 Matthew 9:27 agrees with the Mark account—seemingly in contradiction to what Luke wrote.

47 Thomas Maugh II, "Biblical Pool Uncovered in Jerusalem," *The Los Angeles Times*, August 9, 2005, A-8.

48 W. F. Albright, "Archaeological Discovery and the Scriptures," *Christianity Today*, June 21, 1968, 3.

49 Millar Burrows, *What Mean These Stones?* As quoted by Howard Vos, *Beginnings in Bible Archaeology* (Chicago: Moody Press, 1973), 106.

CHAPTER 4:

The Testimony of Fulfilled Prophecy

50 Carl Henry, *Living Quotations for Christians*, edited by Sherwood Eliot Wirt and Kersten Beckstrom (New York: Harper & Row, 1974), 191.

51 Fulfilled prophecy and mathematical probabilities are from Peter W. Stoner's *Science Speaks Out* (Chicago: Moody Press), 1963.

52 D. James Kennedy, *Why I Believe* (Waco, TX: Word, 1981), 16.

53 Jack Fellman, "Eliezer Ben-Yehuda and the Revival of Hebrew," http://www.jewishvirtuallibrary.org/jsource/biography/ben_yehuda.html.

54 Harry Rimmer, *Palestine: The Coming Storm Center* (Grand Rapids: Eerdmans, 1941).

CHAPTER 5:

The Truce with Science

55 Lee Strobel, *The Case for a Creator* (Grand Rapids: Zondervan, 2004), 346.

56 Richard Dawkins as quoted by Brad Holland, "God vs. Science," *Time*, November 13, 2006, 52.

57 Francis Collins, as quoted by Brad Holland, *Ibid.*, 53.

58 Charles Townes, *Think* (published by IBM, volume 32, March-April, 1966). Used by permission of the author.

59 Charles Darwin in *Origins* as quoted by Ray Bohlin, "Darwin's Black Box," www.leaderu.com/orgs/probe/docs/darwinbx.html, Oct. 10, 2006.

60 Lee Strobel, *The Case for a Creator*, 248.

61 Townes, *Think*, used by permission of the author.

62 John Horgan, *National Geographic*, "Francis Collins—The Scientist as Believer," February, 2007, 33.

63 Genesis 1:1, 1:21, and 1:27.

64 There is no consensus among Christians and neither does the Bible state precisely that the six days of creation are literal 24 hour periods, creative periods of time, or whether an indefinite period of time elapsed between Genesis 1:1 and 2.

65 Samuel J. Alibrando, *Nature Never Stops Talking* (Reedley, CA: Tsaba House, 2005), 124 and Jennifer Kahn, *National Geographic*, "Mending Broken Hearts," February, 2007, 46.

66 www.emc.maricopa.edu/faculty/farabee/BIOBK/BioBookNERV.html, November 1, 2006.

67 Genesis 1:27.

68 Paul Brand and Phillip Yancey, *In His Image* (Grand Rapids: Zondervan Publishing House, 1984), 32.

69 Robert J. Schadewald, *Science Digest*, 1980 as quoted http://www.lhup.edu/DSIMANEK/fe-scidi.html.

70 www.firstbaptisthenderson.org/10reasons.html.

71 CNN, Wednesday, July 23, 2003; posted at www.cnn.com at 12:29 AM EDT.

72 While some of the most reliable Greek manuscripts do not contain the word blood (*haimatos*), other manuscripts have that word, including those used by the King James translators of the seventeenth century, and the use of that word flies in the face of racial prejudice held in their day, that various races of people have different blood.

73 Nigel Brush, *The Limitations of Scientific Truth* (Grand Rapids: Kregel, 2005), 13.

74 For a discussion of Wernher von Braun's religious beliefs see "Plain Talk From von Braun," *Life*, vol. 34, no. 21, Nov. 18, 1957, 136 and *Time*, June 27, 1977, 71.

75 Robert Jastrow, "Have Astronomers found God?" *Reader's Digest*, July 1980, 53.

CHAPTER 6:
The Living Book That Changes Lives

76 Soren Kierkegaard as quoted by George Sweeting, *Who Said That?* (Chicago: Moody Press, 1995), 65.

77 Viggo Olsen, *The Agnostic Who Dared to Search* (Chicago: Moody Press, 1990), 13.

78 Olsen, Ibid., 62, 63.

79 C. S. Lewis, *A Grief Observed* (New York: Harper Collins, 1961), 8.

80 *The Orange County Register*, December 12, 1999, Commentary, 4.

CHAPTER 7:
The Implications of Uncertainty

81 Isaac Taylor as quoted by Warren Wiersbe, *With the Word* (Nashville: Thomas Nelson, 1991), 521.

82 As quoted by Ravi Zacharias, *Walking from East to West* (Grand Rapids: Zondervan, 2006), 173.

83 W. H. Murray understood the importance of commitment. Taken prisoner by the Nazis in World War 2, for three years he was moved from one POW camp to another, but during that

time he began writing a draft of a book on mountaineering on the only paper that was available—rough toilet paper. The Gestapo found the draft and destroyed it. Undaunted, he began the task again in spite of the fact he was living on a starvation diet and so weak he was quite certain he would never climb again. His rewritten manuscript was eventually published in 1947.

84 http://www.gurteen.com/gurteen/gurteen.nsf/id/X00006CB6/, October 16, 2006.

ABOUT THE AUTHOR

Meet **HAROLD SALA** and
Guidelines International Ministries

26161 Marguerite Parkway, Suite F,
Mission Viejo, CA 92679, USA
Email: info@guidelines.org

About Harold . . .

HAROLD J. SALA, who holds a PhD in English Bible from Bob Jones University, is a well known speaker, author and Bible teacher, and has served as founder of Guidelines International, Inc., since 1963, serving as President until 2016, when he relinquished the leadership of the organization to his daughter, Bonnie Sala.

Dr. Sala continues to be a guest lecturer and teacher at universities such as the International Graduate School of Leadership and Asian Theological Seminary in Manila and Donetsk Christian University in Ukraine, national and international conferences, seminars, and churches.

Over 69 books and hundreds of publications have been written by Dr. Sala. Select ones have been published in more than a dozen languages.

For additional information about Guidelines visit their web site at *www.guidelines.org.*

About the Ministry of Guidelines . . .

On September 2, 1963, Harold and Darlene started Guidelines with the release of is first five-minute radio commentary on KFSG in Los Angeles, California. In 1974, the Sala family moved to the Philippines and began their first overseas ministry, working with Far East Broadcasting Co.

Upon return to the US, the Salas branched out to publications in various languages and television production. VCD and DVD production eventually replaced television production. B&H Publishers, Moody Press, Thomas Nelson, Harvest House, Barbour Publishing, Inc., Christian Publications, Inc., and OMF Literature, Inc. are some of the publishers and distributors of the Salas' books and booklets.

Harold and Darlene train pastors and do conferences targeting families, which also singles, professionals and various groups, and speak at churches in the United States as well as the Philippines, China, Ukraine, Russia and countries throughout Europe. Financial assistance for about 30 pastors is also distributed to help continue the ministry of the Word.

Now in its 55th year of ministry, the Guidelines radio commentary is now carried on over 1,000 outlets in 19 languages and is heard in 49 of the 50 states in the U.S. Harold and Darlene have been married since 1959. They have three married children and eight grandchildren.